C000059803

NOT MANY PEOPLE KNOW IT'S 1988!

Michael Caine's

File of Facts

Royalties to the
National Playing Fields Association

GUILD PUBLISHING LONDON

Cartoons by Larry.

Designed by Harold King.

This edition published 1987 by
Book Club Associates by arrangement with
Robson Books.

Printed in Great Britain by
Biddles Ltd, Guildford and King's Lynn.

THIS IS 1988!

January

M		4	11	18	25
T		5	12	19	26
W		6	13	20	27
T		7	14	21	28
F	1	8	15	22	29
S	2	9	16	23	30
S	3	10	17	24	31

February

M	1	8	15	22	29
T	2	9	16	23	
W	3	10	17	24	
T	4	11	18	25	
F	5	12	19	26	
S	6	13	20	27	
S	7	14	21	28	

March

M		7	14	21	28
T	1	8	15	22	29
W	2	9	16	23	30
T	3	10	17	24	31
F	4	11	18	25	
S	5	12	19	26	
S	6	13	20	27	

April

M		4	11	18	25
T		5	12	19	26
W		6	13	20	27
T		7	14	21	28
F	1	8	15	22	29
S	2	9	16	23	30
S	3	10	17	24	

May

M	30	2	9	16	23
T	31	3	10	17	24
W		4	11	18	25
T		5	12	19	26
F		6	13	20	27
S		7	14	21	28
S	1	8	15	22	29

June

M		6	13	20	27
T		7	14	21	28
W	1	8	15	22	29
T	2	9	16	23	30
F	3	10	17	24	
S	4	11	18	25	
S	5	12	19	26	

July

M		4	11	18	25
T		5	12	19	26
W		6	13	20	27
T		7	14	21	28
F	1	8	15	22	29
S	2	9	16	23	30
S	3	10	17	24	31

August

M	1	8	15	22	29
T	2	9	16	23	30
W	3	10	17	24	31
T	4	11	18	25	
F	5	12	19	26	
S	6	13	20	27	
S	7	14	21	28	

September

M		5	12	19	26
T		6	13	20	27
W		7	14	21	28
T	1	8	15	22	29
F	2	9	16	23	30
S	3	10	17	24	
S	4	11	18	25	

October

M	31	3	10	17	24
T		4	11	18	25
W		5	12	19	26
T		6	13	20	27
F		7	14	21	28
S	1	8	15	22	29
S	2	9	16	23	30

November

M		7	14	21	28
T	1	8	15	22	29
W	2	9	16	23	30
T	3	10	17	24	
F	4	11	18	25	
S	5	12	19	26	
S	6	13	20	27	

December

M		5	12	19	26
T		6	13	20	27
W		7	14	21	28
T	1	8	15	22	29
F	2	9	16	23	30
S	3	10	17	24	31
S	4	11	18	25	

Introduction

1988 is an extraordinary year. There's not a single day that doesn't commemorate something intriguing or odd that's occurred in the past. You'll discover that the last Japanese soldier surrendered World War II on 10 March — in 1974. And if you turn to 6 August you'll find that Archbishop Matthew Parker was born 484 years ago. His huge conk and habit of snooping on people earned him a nickname that's guaranteed him a place in posterity — Nosey Parker. On 20 June a year ago the world's longest sausage was cooked in Hyde Park — all 9.8 miles of it. And if you're looking for something to celebrate on 23 June you'll find that it's the third anniversary of the world's first official dromedary dairy.

Nuggets of odd information like this are a great way of brightening up an ordinary day — and they're useful too. When I was just a Cockney kid going to school in Peckham I was known as the Professor because I spent so much time reading. That could have been a problem, but because I always had a collection of strange facts I earned my place in the local gang. And an amazing fact is always useful when it comes to cheering people up or taking the wind out of some know-all's sails.

For me one of the high points of 1988 will be Christmas. I'm the Sam Spiegel of Christmas — I put on a really big production every year. To me Christmas is the most important of all festivals; I adore it. From September onwards all my energy and effort goes into preparation and we have a big celebration on Christmas Day with all the family and lots of friends. It's the one day of the year when everyone should be happy.

I'll be having a good time the rest of the year too. Everything I do, whether it's making movies, travelling, creating a country home here in England, I do because I thoroughly enjoy it. I think I'm the laziest man in the world; I wouldn't get out of bed unless I had something interesting to do each day. But there's so much that's interesting and fascinating in my life that I get up at dawn just to fit it all in. And finding nuggets of amazing information to add to my collection of knowledge is just one more reason I find life so enjoyable.

Something that never fails to surprise me is that the more fascinated you are about the odd things in life, the more curious are the things you discover. In 1985 I made a film called *Mona Lisa*. I did it mainly as a favour to Bob Hoskins, who's an old friend, and the director, Neil Jordan, because I wanted to get a bit of notice for a good British movie. Now, here's something that really amazed me. The production office of *Mona Lisa* was in St Olave's Hospital in Bermondsey, which had been converted into an office building. I was born in St Olave's in 1933. I reckon that makes me the first actor in history to have made a film from the hospital where I was born. Not many people know that!

Have a good year!

Michael Caine

P.S. This book is being published in aid of the National Playing Fields Association which does great work in creating and maintaining parks and open space for kids to play in. If you want to know more about the charity and its important aims, turn to back of book.

JANUARY 1988

1
FRIDAY

15 years ago today Britain became a member of the E.E.C. and began to participate in the European Parliament. Each year the Parliament produces 100 million pages of reports in seven languages; stacked on top of each other, they would make a pile 14 times the height of Big Ben.

And did you know that . . .
6,000 new chemicals are added to the lists of the American Chemical Society each week?

2
SATURDAY

King Zog of Albania fled his country 42 years ago today and became the last monarch of the nation. His habit of smoking more than a hundred cigarettes a day was once celebrated on a postage stamp.

Today in 1869 the world's first traffic light, situated near Parliament Square, London, exploded and injured the policeman operating it. It remained the only traffic light in the city until others were introduced 50 years later.

And did you know that . . .
Jerome K. Jerome's middle name was Klapka?

3
SUNDAY

The first drinking straw was patented 100 years ago today.

And today in 1983 while South African Prime Minister Botha announced on the radio that the following Wednesday there would be a national day of prayer for an end to the drought, a cloudburst hit Delmas in the Transvaal and drowned 100,000 chickens.

And did you know that . . .
When Walt Disney released One Hundred and One Dalmatians *the price of Dalmatian puppies in the US increased by 400%?*

NOTES

1 January: New Year's Day — Public holiday UK and Republic of Ireland.

On New Year's Resolutions...

I don't make New Year's Resolutions – for me every day can be January 1. I have a trick; no matter how outlandish or how far off or how expensive or unattainable anything is, I write it down on a list and I don't rest until I've achieved it. Some of them take years. Five years ago in Los Angeles I wrote down 'Start my own production company in England'. It'll take another three years, but I'll get there!

JANUARY 1988

4 MONDAY

General Tom Thumb was born 150 years ago today. His maximum adult height was 40 inches but lack of stature never held him back. As the star of Barnum's circus he became the toast of New York and he won the heart of Queen Victoria who insisted on no fewer than three audiences with him. After that he became known as 'the Pet of the Palace'.

And did you know that . . .
The average human brain uses as much electricity as a 10-watt electric light bulb?

5 TUESDAY

Today in 1797 the first man to wear a top hat was arrested and fined for wearing an item of apparel likely to cause alarm to anyone of a nervous disposition.

In the Catholic calendar today is St Simeon Stylites' Day. St Simeon proved his devotion to God by living for 37 years on top of a pillar.

And did you know that . . .
Muscular strength reaches a peak at the age of 25 – after that it goes into decline?

6 WEDNESDAY

Today is Christmas Day – well, it was until 1752 when Britain adopted the Gregorian calendar and 25 December became the new Christmas Day. On the Shetland Isle of Foula they've stuck to the original Julian calendar and still celebrate later than the rest of the country. The change of date from January to December explains some of the traditions associated with Christmas – snow, for example. We very rarely have snow in December, but in January, at the 'old' Christmas, it's quite common.

7 THURSDAY

The first baby to be born on the continent of Antarctica came into the world 10 years ago today.

Five years ago today 53-year-old Giovanni Vigilotto went on trial in Phoenix, Arizona and admitted that he had married at least 82 women in the last 20 years.

And did you know that . . .
The Russian postal service will not deliver letters containing chewing gum?

8
FRIDAY

Today in 1935 the King was born – Elvis Presley. The son of poor sharecropper parents, he amassed a huge fortune which was only fully revealed on his death. Among the contents of his mansion, Graceland, was a collection of statues of the Venus de Milo, one of which came posed against an electric waterfall, eight cars, 18 television sets and a hundred pairs of trousers.

And did you know that . . .
The average new-born baby spends 133 minutes a day crying?

9
SATURDAY

Richard Nixon, disgraced American president, was born today in 1913. He was once signing copies of his book *Six Crises* in a shop when a man came up and bought one. Nixon asked who he should address the inscription to. 'That's your seventh crisis,' smiled the customer. 'My name is Stanislaus Wojechzleschki.'

Gyspy Rose Lee, who gave pleasure to millions with her striptease act, was born today in 1914. In a New York auction one of her admirers lashed out $500 for her mink G-string.

And did you know that . . .
According to research at Exeter University, one in six burglars has been burgled?

10
SUNDAY

140 years ago today the Penny Post was introduced by Rowland Hill. He also invented envelopes and stamps to go on them, and the system was completed when the novelist Anthony Trollope invented the post-box.

And did you know that . . .
The 'golden' Oscars are made of 92% tin?
On average, dogs in the city live longer than those in the country?

NOTES

_____

_____

_____

_____

_____

JANUARY 1988

11
MONDAY

60 years ago the novelist Thomas Hardy died. He'd asked to buried at Stinsford in Dorset but his admirers preferred a burial with honours in Westminster Abbey. It was decided to bury his ashes in London and his heart in Dorset, and after the service his sister returned to the country with the poet's heart in a casket. Unfortunately she left it on the kitchen table and her cat ran off with it. It was never found.

And did you know that . . .
Transylvania was the first country to declare religious freedom?

12
TUESDAY

Twelve years ago today that great crime writer Dame Agatha Christie died. During the run of her play *The Mousetrap*, which is still going strong, the wardobe mistress has calculated that she has ironed more than 36 miles of shirts.

And did you know that . . .
Experts estimate that of all life forms known to have inhabited the earth, only 10% exist today?
   It take 43 muscles to frown but only 17 to smile?

13
WEDNESDAY

Windscreen wipers were introduced for the first time today in 1921.
   Charles Perrault, who wrote the orignal fairytales of *Cinderella* and *Puss in Boots* was born today in 1628. In his version of *Cinderella* the slipper that Cinders loses was made of fur, not glass.

And did you know that . . .
While you've been reading this sentence 50,000,000 of the cells in your body will have died and been replaced?

14
THURSDAY

Four years ago today Ray Kroc, founder of the McDonald's hamburger empire, died. There are nearly 8,000 McDonald's outlets in 32 countries with sales totalling more than $8 billion in 1984. Kroc established a university where students can study for a degree in Hamburgerology and it's claimed in America that through his McDonald's franchises he's made millionaires of more people than anyone else in history.

And did you know that . . .
Cleopatra's real name was Auletes?

JANUARY 1988

15 FRIDAY

Prohibition hit America today in 1920, but no one told the U.S Department of Agriculture about it and they continued to distribute instructions for making alcohol from apples, bananas and other fruit. The longest period of prohibition on record is surprisingly short – just 26 years in Iceland from 1908 to 1934.

And did you know that . . .
If the descendants of a single pair of flies survived they would number over 335 trillion after five months?

16 SATURDAY

Today in 1963 the last of the *Bonanza* series was run on American television.

In 1547 Tsar Ivan IV was crowned and set about establishing the reputation that caused him to be named Ivan the Terrible. He claimed to have deflowered a thousand virgins and killed as many of his own children.

And did you know that . . .
At one Mexican prison there is a rule that a guard must serve the remainder of the sentence of any prisoner who escapes?

17 SUNDAY

British breakfast television celebrates its fifth birthday today. Everyone said it wouldn't last, but 'Breakfast Time' is still going strong.

Benjamin Franklin and Muhammad Ali were both born today, Franklin in 1706 and Ali in 1942. As well as being a national leader Ben Franklin invented the lightning conductor, bifocal lenses and a new kind of rocking chair, and fought to establish the first fire department, hospital, lending library, postal system and fire insurance company in America.

And did you know that . . .
30% of the meat sold in the US goes to make hamburgers and McDonald's sells more than three billion burgers a year?

NOTES

On Writing...

I'm very interested in writing. Everyone asks when I'm going to write my autobiography; I'm not, but I *am* going to write fiction – modern stuff, thrillers, that kind of thing, like Dashiell Hammett and Raymond Chandler whom I admire.   (12 January)

JANUARY 1988

18 MONDAY

106 years ago A.A. Milne, creator of Winnie-the-Pooh, Piglet and Christopher Robin, was born. Milne's books have been translated into dozens of languages, including Latin, and a share of the royalties from them forms a vital part of the income of the Garrick Club.

Five years ago today Sotheby's confirmed that a valuable pot, thought to be the work of potter Bernard Leach, was in fact a forgery. It had been made by an inmate of Featherstone Jail during his pottery lesson.

And did you know that . . .
Walt Disney is the only Hollywood producer to be honoured with a postage stamp?

19 TUESDAY

35 years ago today Lucille Ball gave birth to a real-life son, Desi Arnaz, and a fictional one, Ricky Ricardo, in the 'I Love Lucy' TV series.

And did you know that . . .
In Zambia the Securicor security company equips its guards with bows and arrows which, it's speculated, could be poison-tipped?
The Navajo language was used to create an unbreakable code by the Americans during World War II?

20 WEDNESDAY

10 years ago today an Athens court decreed the official price of viriginity to be £4,600.

In 1892 the first game of basketball, invented by James Naismith, was played in Massachusetts.

Shipping tycoon Aristotle Onassis was born today in 1902. Despite his popular image he was not Greek but Turkish.

And did you know that . . .
Shoes worn on the right foot wear out faster than shoes on the left foot?

21 THURSDAY

Taxi-cabs were officially recognised in London for the first time today in 1906.

In 1793 King Lous XVI went to the guillotine, a piece of equipment which he had himself helped design. Perhaps his greatest legacy was the handkerchief, which before his reign was just a scrap of cloth of any shape or size. It was Louis who decreed that hankies everywhere should be square.

JANUARY 1988

22
FRIDAY

Today in 1901 Queen Victoria died, the longest-reigning of all British monarchs and the one who saw most change. Among her achievements, she was the first British monarch to have her photo taken, use a lift, a telephone and travel on a train.

And did you know that . . .
The word 'bride' comes from an ancient German word meaning 'the one who cooks'?

23
SATURDAY

10 years ago today Sweden became the first country to ban aerosol cans. Also 10 years ago, a dog shot a boy dead in Japan by accidentally triggering a loaded shotgun with its leg.

And did you know that . . .
In sixteenth-century France vine weevils were put on trial for destroying crops?
*   The term 'bootlegging' started in the days of the Wild West when Indians would carry whisky (sold to them illegally) in their boots?*

24
SUNDAY

Today in 1965 Winston Churchill died after a long decline. In his eighties, when it was widely rumoured that he was senile, he made a visit to the House of Commons and his arrival caused something of a stir. 'They say he's dotty,' commented one MP as the former prime minister passed. 'They say he can't hear either,' commented Churchill.

And did you know that . . .
There are more than 17 miles of corridors in the Pentagon?

NOTES

_____

_____

_____

_____

_____

JANUARY 1988

25 MONDAY

Today in 1941 mobster Al Capone died. With the help of his gang he was believed to have amassed more than $100,000,000 from gambling, illegal liquor and extortion, yet the only crime for which he was successfully prosecuted was tax evasion. Instead of dying in a hail of bullets, as might have been expected, he was killed by syphilis – despite being the first sufferer to be treated with antibiotics.

And did you know that . . .
The skin accounts for around 16% of total body weight?

26 TUESDAY

Today in 1926 Logie Baird gave the first demonstration of his new invention, television. No one who saw it was very impressed! Sometimes television fiction is stranger than fact. Take the popular 'Six Million Dollar Man' series. One biochemist was inspired to work out what it would cost to make a man and priced human components with the aid of a biochemicals catalogue. By the time he'd finished, the price was almost exactly six million dollars!

And did you know that . . .
An attempt to kill Fidel Castro with a poisoned chocolate milkshake went wrong because the assassin put the drink in the freezer and froze it solid?

27 WEDNESDAY

Today in 1756 Wolfgang Amadeus Mozart, the greatest musical genius the world has known, was born. His brilliance astounded everyone who heard him. In Rome during Holy Week each year people flocked to hear Gregario's *Miserere* performed by the Papal choir. It was the only chance they had to hear it because the Pope jealously guarded the music and refused to allow it to be performed elsewhere. Mozart heard it once, then went home and wrote out the whole long and complicated score from memory.

And did you know that . . .
Of all the thousands of hymns that have been written, the average churchgoer knows only 150?

28 THURSDAY

Today in 1896 the first motorist to be convicted of a speeding offence on British roads appeared in court. He'd been spotted doing 8 m.p.h. in a 2 m.p.h. area and had to suffer the humiliation of being chased and overtaken by a policeman – on a bicycle.

JANUARY 1988

29 FRIDAY

Today in 1879 W.C. Fields was born. He was so worried about losing his cash that wherever he went he opened bank accounts. They weren't all in his own name, either. Among his pseudonyms were Aristotle Hoop, Ludovic Fishpond and Figley E. Whitesides. Many of these accounts still exist because Fields didn't keep complete records and forgot to close them.

And did you know that . . .
The English language has more words than any other?

30 SATURDAY

Led by Karl Wallenda and consisting mainly of family members, the Great Wallendas were the most spectacular tight-rope walking act the world has seen. Their most amazing achievement was a seven-person pyramid, performed without a safety net. 26 years ago tonight, during a performance in Detroit, disaster struck and the pyramid toppled. Two members were killed, one paralysed and Karl Wallenda was seriously injured.

And did you know that . . .
Many people wear false teeth containing radioactive uranium which makes the teeth gleam even in artifical light?

31 SUNDAY

New York has always celebrated parades through its streets in a very distinctive style, with tons of ticker-tape being showered from the windows of tall office buildings. These days with computers taking over from the old ticker machines there's sometimes an embarrassing lack of tape. When the Iran hostages paraded through the streets of New York seven years ago today 100 miles of tape had to be brought in from a firm in Connecticut.

85 years ago Tallulah Bankhead, famous for her outrageous wit and style, was born. She once dropped a fifty-dollar note into a tambourine held by a Salvation Army officer with the words, 'Don't bother to thank me. I know what a perfectly ghastly season it's been for you Spanish dancers.'

NOTES

On Television...

I don't watch a lot of TV but when I do I like it to be good. And I don't work on TV –I have this rule! Never appear anywhere where people can watch you for nothing!

(3 January)

FEBRUARY 1988

1 MONDAY

According to a Madame Tussaud's poll published 4 years ago, David Bowie was the most popular waxwork figure in the exhibition. Margaret Thatcher was the favourite poltician, and the most hated people were Adolf Hitler, Colonel Qaddafi and Ronald Reagan.

Also 4 years ago, the sailboard or windsurfer was officially declared a British invention.

And did you know that . . .
It takes 492 seconds for sunlight to reach the Earth?

2 TUESDAY

Today in 1984 it was announced that the halfpenny was to be scrapped. There had been a coin of this denomination in use since 1280.

106 years ago today James Joyce was born in Dublin. Not many people know that the word 'quark', used by scientists to describe hypothetical particles, was adopted from Joyce's book *Finnegan's Wake*.

And did you know that . . .
A baby born in Argentina with two heads was given two christenings?
More than 400 million bottles of whisky are drunk in Japan each year – equivalent to more than three bottles for each man, woman and child?

3 WEDNESDAY

29 years ago today rock star Buddy Holly was tragically killed in an aircrash in Iowa. When his body was found his spectacles were missing. Twenty years later someone found a pair of glasses without lenses in the area of the crash and they were identified as Buddy's.

Four years ago today newspaper articles reported the fate of an attempt by the French to develop a contraceptive ointment for men. Apparently the girlfriends of the lusty subjects of experiment were absorbing some of the hormones that their boyfriends were rubbing on and had begun to develop moustaches.

And did you know that . . .
Lord Byron resorted to curlers to give him romantically wavy hair?

4 THURSDAY

Taxi-drivers in Greece were banned from discussing with their passengers anything except subjects related to their work today in 1984 after rows about politics had stopped traffic in Athens.

FEBRUARY 1988

5
FRIDAY

35 years ago today Walt Disney's version of *Peter Pan* was released. Unable to decide how to portray Fairy Tinkerbell, the animators looked around for a face and figure that would represent the best of American womanhood. Eventually Tinkerbell's vital statistics were based on those of Marilyn Monroe.

Four years ago today in Nairobi a 100-year-old man was married to a 14-year-old girl. The best man was a stripling of 86.

And did you know that . . .
Jimmy Durante's nose was once insured for $140,000?

6
SATURDAY

Ronald Reagan is 77 today! He's the only American President to have shared his bed with a monkey and have his polyps discussed on TV. Not that he wanted to be President in the first place. In 1973 he said, 'The thought of being President frightens me and I do not think I want the job.'

18 years ago today Mary Quant predicted that pubic hair would become a fashionable adornment and revealed that her husband trimmed *hers* into a heart-shape.

And did you know that . . .
In the 1960s it was revealed that the then Duke of Devonshire numbered among his relatives the Governor of the Bank of England, the Prime Minister, the President of the United States and Fred Astaire?

7
SUNDAY

Charles Dickens was born 176 years ago today. Although the sheer size and weight of his books have gained him a reputation for being a serious person, he in fact had a zany sense of the ridiculous. In one of his houses he had a hidden door built into his study. It was disguised by rows of shelves containing fake books and he took delight in inventing ridiculous names for these dummies. Among them were *Noah's Arkitecture*, *The Quarrelly Review* and *The Virtues of Our Ancestors*, a book so thin that there was scarcely room for the title.

And did you know that . . .
The tulip was named after its resemblance to a turban and was originally known as tulipan?

NOTES

On Ronald Reagan...

It's nice to know there's another role open for movie actors at the end of their careers...
(6 February)

FEBRUARY 1988

8 MONDAY

Five years ago today the IRA staged their strangest kidnapping and made off with Shergar, the Derby-winning racehorse belonging to the Aga Khan. The £2-million ransom they demanded was not paid and nothing has been seen of the horse since.

Four years ago today brave Bruce McCandless stepped out of his spacecraft without a safety line and became the first man to fly untethered in space. Fortunately his jet-powered backpack worked and he was able to return safely to Earth.

And did you know that . . .
In the six months after its introduction, 72 million Penny Black stamps were sold?

9 TUESDAY

Today in 1984 the only known gay funeral parlour, staffed by gays and catering exclusively for gays, was reported to have opened in San Francisco.

And did you know that . . .
The weight of the Earth increases by around 100,000lb each year, mainly due to meteor dust falling from the sky?
Some Persian carpets have more than 300 knots per square inch?

10 WEDNESDAY

Dr Alex Comfort, author of *The Joy of Sex*, is 68 today. During research his fellow sexologist Alfred Kinsey encountered a man who had had sex nearly five times a day for more than 30 years; the average number of times, according to Kinsey, was 2.3 times a week.

And did you know that . . .
You need about one calorie to read 650 words?

11 THURSDAY

10 years ago today red-frocked cardinals gathered in Rome for the inauguration of Pope John Paul II. At the age of 57 he was quite young as Popes go but, even so, he couldn't rival the record of Benedict IX, who became Pope at the age of 11.

And did you know that . . .
The cockroach has existed, unchanged, for around 250 million years?

FEBRUARY 1988

FRIDAY

Tom Keating, the man who threw the art world into chaos when it was revealed that he had produced more than 2,000 fakes which had been snapped up by dealers and experts, died four years ago today. Ironically, shortly before his death he recorded a series of TV programmes showing how to imitate the styles and techniques of famous painters.

And did you know that . . .
During their lifetime most people eat food equivalent to the weight of six elephants?

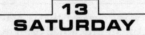
SATURDAY

296 years ago the Campbells tried to wipe out the Macdonalds in the Glencoe Massacre. To this day the nine of diamonds is known as the Curse of Scotland because the marks on the card bear a resemblance to the arms of the Master of Stair, who was held responsible for the slaughter.

And did you know that . . .
The largest bell in the world is housed in the Kremlin, but has not been tolled since 1736?

14
SUNDAY

Today is St Valentine's Day – though which St Valentine is not clear. There are at least two St Valentines on record, one of them a Roman priest who was beheaded in the third century AD. Bits of various St Valentines are found throughout Europe, including two bodies and a head in Spain, a body in Rome and another head elsewhere in Italy. Take your pick! No one's sure how St Valentine came to be the patron saint of romance, but there may be some confusion with the Norman word *galentine* which means 'a ladies' man'.

A survey published three years ago reveals the statistical side of love and marriage. Apparently the average engagement for couples in Great Britain lasted 19 months, girls in Lancashire had more expensive engagement rings than those in East Anglia, the average wedding cost £2,000, and 20 per cent of couples have the ceremony videoed.

NOTES

FEBRUARY 1988

15
MONDAY

Today in 1976 the price of the long French loaf known as a *baguette*, a staple part of the French diet, was increased by the government to 1 franc – at today's prices, around 12p.

And did you know that . . .
The Swiss navy was invited to the opening of the Panama Canal? There is no Swiss navy!
  Camel-hair brushes are not made from camel hair?

16
TUESDAY

33 years ago today it was revealed that a new mountain had been discovered in Siberia. Apparently it had been overlooked – all 24,000 feet of it.

And did you know that . . .
  The Romans used weasels to catch mice in the way we use cats?
  In 1975 the inhabitants of Philadelphia voted a dead man to the city council because there had not been time to remove his name from the ballot papers?

17
WEDNESDAY

Seven years ago today reports that a talking cow had been discovered in Bangalore excited thousands of Indians. The owner of the cow accepted a fee from a television company to appear with his amazing animal and the nation held its breath. It needn't have bothered – the cow didn't talk.

And did you know that . . .
A Texas man who was born without ears – or even ear-holes – was able to hear through his mouth?
  Tenterhooks were originally used for stretching cloth?

18
THURSDAY

424 years ago today Michelangelo, the great Renaissance painter, sculptor and poet died. Poet? Yes – not many people know that he left 300 poems, nor that he signed only one of his many works, the *Pietà* that stands in St Peter's. And he only put his name on that because he heard a bunch of Renaissance tourists telling each other that it was the work of another sculptor.

And did you know that . . .
Many Greek statues and buildings, now considered the model of unadorned simplicity, were originally covered in gaudy paint?

FEBRUARY 1988

19
FRIDAY

Prince Andrew, the Duke of York, Royal Navy high-flier and Falklands veteran, is 28 today. It's not on record whether he likes Mars bars, but when the QE2 set sail for the South Atlantic during the campaign she carried on board a cache of three million Mars bars. A journalist worked out that if anyone had bothered to lay them end to end they would have stretched for 200 miles.

And did you know that . . .

A 1983 survey of Dutch women discovered that 12 per cent of those taking oral contraceptives couldn't be sure that they'd remembered to take the Pill the day before?

20
SATURDAY

Four years ago today it was reported that a Swedish dentist in Karlskrona had found a sprouting tomato seed in a patient's gum. He took it out and planted it in a pot, but it died.

And did you know that . . .

When someone dies in Turkey, the mourners wear violet, not black?

Research shows that in 1979 the average American was being bombarded by more than 500 adverts each day?

21
SUNDAY

Identity cards issued during the Second World War were scrapped 36 years ago today. Many years before that – 310 to be precise – three men were hanged on Greenberry Hill, known these days as Primrose Hill, in London. Their names were Green, Berry and Hill.

And did you know that . . .

The dogs most likely to make good guide dogs, including labradors and Alsatians, are the dogs most likely to go blind themselves?

NOTES

On France...

France is the foreign country I love best. It has style about everything and it's proud of itself. They have the greatest wine in the world, the greatest food, the greatest fashion, the greatest chic. The French could give the British lessons in patriotism and chauvinism!

(15 February)

FEBRUARY 1988

22
MONDAY

256 years ago today George Washington died. As well as being the first President of the USA he was also the first American millionaire. His is commemorated on July 4 each year in the small town of George, Washington, where they bake a massive 1,200-pound cherry pie in his memory.

23
TUESDAY

355 years ago today England's most famous diarist, Samuel Pepys, was born. He began his diary in 1660 and only stopped it in 1669 because he thought he was going blind. During the Great Fire of London he buried his Parmesan cheese in a hole in the back garden to keep it safe. On his 36th birthday he celebrated by going to see the mummified body of Catherine de Valois which was kept in Westminster Abbey. After bribing the man who kept watch over her, he kissed her on the lips and fondled her – just as he fondled his maidservant's breasts at home, much to his wife's displeasure.

And did you know that . . .
Uncooked lobsters are dark blue or green in colour and only turn red when boiled?

24
WEDNESDAY

179 years ago today Richard Brinsley Sheridan, playwright, MP and manager of the Drury Lane Theatre, was summoned to Covent Garden because the theatre had caught fire. He went, saw for himself that the place was burning to the ground, and then retired to a coffee house nearby where he ordered a bottle of port. When a friend remarked that he was taking the bad news well he replied, 'A man may surely be allowed to take a glass of wine by his own fireside.'

25
THURSDAY

74 years ago today John Arlott, Britain's best-loved cricket commentator, was born. The sound of his voice is enough to evoke memories of long summer afternoons and the civilized sound of leather on willow. Less evocative are some of the slips of the tongue that have amused radio listeners over the years; during one match a commentator announced to the waiting millions, 'The bowler's Holding, the batsman's Willey.'

And did you know that . . .
A West Indian limbo expert has danced her way under a bar only 6.5 inches from the ground?

FEBRUARY 1988

26
FRIDAY

William F. Cody, otherwise known as Buffalo Bill, was born 122 years ago today. Despite his nickname he hunted bison and not buffalo! He was also very keen on whisky, but was careful not to let his drinking habits get out of hand by limiting himself to just one glass a day. Mind you, that glass held a pint.

And did you know that . . .
After his death the body of the fattest man who ever lived was transported to his funeral in a furniture van?

27
SATURDAY

Today in 1965 Goldie the eagle caused some excitement after escaping from the aviary at London Zoo and roosting in Regent's Park, where thousands of ornithologists and sightseers gathered to watch him. He's probably the first bird to have made the front cover of the popular newspapers for a whole fortnight.

And did you know that . . .
Leonardo da Vinci created designs for a flush toilet and a helicopter hundreds of years before they were produced?

28
SUNDAY

Three years ago Prince Charles made history by becoming the first royal blood donor.

And did you know that . . .
Many Russian maps used to show Moscow a few miles away from its actual position to confuse guided missiles?
The French drink 100 bottles of wine per head of population per year? The British drink 13.

NOTES

_____

_____

_____

_____

_____

FEBRUARY 1988

196 years ago today composer Gioacchino Rossini was born. His most famous opera is *The Barber of Seville*; others were not so well-received. In 1826 *The Siege of Corinth* was greeted with hostility by the critics and to one Rossini replied with scathing wit: 'Sir, I am sitting in the smallest room of my house. I have your review before me. In a moment it will be behind me.'

And did you know that . . .

11BC was the last year to have a February 30, thanks to Augustus Caesar's reorganization of the calendar?

The 365-day year was established by Julius Caesar in 45BC, with an extra day added to every fourth February to even things up. Unfortunately when he died there was a mix-up and every February contained 30 days. When Augustus Caesar became emperor in 27BC, the seasons were several days off schedule. Something had to be done, and Augustus eliminated three leap years to allow the calendar to catch up. As a tribute to himself he scrapped the month known as Sextilius *and called it August.* Sextilius *had had only thirty days, which was not enough for the Emperor's liking, so he stole a day from February and thus made it the shortest month of the year!*

NOTES

On Theatre Critics...

I haven't done theatre for 25 years and all it means to me is a tremendous amount of hard work, with no money, in order to be smashed by the critics. When you've been a movie star you could give the most brilliant performance in the history of world theatre and you'd still be slated!   (29 February)

THINGS TO DO IN MARCH:

_____

_____

_____

_____

MARCH 1988

1 TUESDAY

Three years ago today the French authorities launched a new attack on the growing use of Franglais by revealing that 200 companies and individuals had been fined for using such words as 'computer', 'cameraman' and 'jumbo jet'. The maximum fine for uttering these words was £54.

And did you know that . . .

According to a recent survey, people who go fishing are more keen on coarse-cut marmalade, Chinese food and Shredded Wheat than average?
A good journalist has a vocabulary of around 15,000 words?

2 WEDNESDAY

There was relief for hungry workers in China today in 1985 when it became compulsory for restaurants in Peking to open at lunchtime.
On the same day it was reported that a Yugoslavian farm worker whose hand was cut off in an accident had had it sewn back on – 65 days later.

And did you know that . . .

The odds against a Royal Flush in poker are 649,739 to 1?
Phobophobia is the term used to describe a fear of fears?
One in ten people in the UK lose all their teeth by the age of 21?

In China in 1900 a wooden statue which slipped off a temple shelf and killed a man who was praying was found guilty of murder and had its head chopped off?
Women in Iceland do not change their names when they marry?

3 THURSDAY

77 years ago today legendary blonde bombshell Jean Harlow was born. She was once introduced to Margot Asquith and, being unfamiliar with the visitor's name asked whether the 't' was pronounced or silent. Margot Asquith looked at her coldly and replied, 'The "t" is silent – as in Harlow.'

And did you know that . . .

More babies are born late at night and in the early hours of the morning than in the afternoon?
Marilyn Monroe once modelled for an advert for Idaho Potatoes?

MARCH 1988

4
FRIDAY

43 years ago today the Queen joined the ATS, where she learnt such useful skills as driving and map-reading. She also learned to service car engines and on the last day of the course her father, George VI, came to watch her at work. No matter what she tried, she couldn't get the engine to start. 'Haven't you fixed it yet?' asked the King, smiling. He had surreptitiously removed the distributor cap.

5
SATURDAY

35 years ago today the Russian dictator Joseph Stalin died. While at the Yalta conference Winston Churchill pointed out to him a statue of a sleeping lion that he liked very much and said that he understood that there was a tradition in Russia of giving the best things as gifts to important guests. 'That's true,' agreed a straight-faced Stalin. 'And the best thing in Russia is socialism.' Churchill never got his lion.

And did you know that . . .
In Siena, Italy, a local law forbids women christened Mary to work as prostitutes?

6
SUNDAY

Three years ago today Ivan Lawrence, MP for Burton-on-Trent, gave the longest Commons speech of the century by holding forth for 4 hours and 23 minutes on the subject of fluoride in tap water.

And did you know that . . .
Racing greyhounds have their noseprints, which are as individual as human fingerprints, kept on record to prevent fraud?
Henry Ford built a car body and steering wheel from soyabeans, which he believed were the way forward for the world?

NOTES

On Royalty...

I think the royal family are a very good thing for this country. I like a head of state, like the Queen, who is separate from the head of politics. It means you can complain about houses or taxes or political things without knocking the state. I can never understand republics – the funny thing is that in France everyone knows who the president is but not the prime minister, and in Israel everyone knows who the prime minister is but no one knows the president! (4 March)

MARCH 1988

7 MONDAY

Kim Ung-Yong was born in Korea 27 years ago today and by the time he was five months old he was talking. Two months later he could read and write. At the age of four he was fluent in three languages and before he was five he'd starred on Japanese TV solving integral calculus maths problems. The experts were stunned and had to admit that his IQ was so high it just couldn't be measured.

And did you know that . . .
The best wood for making pencils is incense cedar?

8 TUESDAY

Five years ago it was reported that the governor of Bangkok Gaol had bought a sub-machine gun and silencer after complaints from the inmates of Death Row that the old gun used for dawn executions was making too much noise and waking them up.

And did you know that . . .
There are more English language teachers in Russia than there are people learning Russian in the USA?
The onion is the most widely-used vegetable in the world?

9 WEDNESDAY

New Zealand is justifiably proud of its equal rights policies – in fact it was the first country to give women the vote. But half the population must have wondered how equal they were when five years ago today a judge ordered the destruction of 2,000 male nude calendars because they were 'an affront to the accepted standard of decency'.

And did you know that . . .
If the history of the Earth was condensed into a hundred years, dinosaurs would have been around three years ago, three weeks ago the first man would have appeared and man would have walked on the moon three-and-a-half seconds ago?

10 THURSDAY

14 years ago today the last Japanese soldier gave up his fight to win the Second World War. Hiro Onoda was sent to the Philippines in 1944 with instructions to wage one-man guerilla warfare if necessary – and that's what he did for the next 29 years. Only when his ex-commanding officer, now a bookseller, was sent out in 1974 to order him to stop fighting did Japan's most loyal soldier call it a day.

And did you know that . . .
Leonardo da Vinci used to do a form of origami?

MARCH 1988

11 FRIDAY

The shortest theatrical run in history took place 58 years ago today. *The Intimate Revue* suffered every first-night problem imaginable. The curtains refused to open, costumes didn't fit, the performers forgot their lines and it took twenty-five minutes to change the scenery between each brief sketch. It was such a disaster that there was no second night.

And did you know that . . .
During the nineteenth century Manhattan was home to the Molasses Gang who mugged their victims by pulling a hat full of treacle over their heads?

12 SATURDAY

Today was the day in 1983 that Luigi Longhi, a Dane with a fascination with women's hair, was sent to a psychiatric prison for an indefinite period. He kidnapped a West German hitch-hiker, tied her up and before strangling her, washed her hair four times.

And did you know that . . .
The Giant African snail breeds so fast that if all the full-grown offspring from a breeding period of three years were lined up nose to tail they would stretch from the Earth to the Moon and back again 1,000,000 times?

13 SUNDAY

Three years ago the enterprising Anita Roddick was named Businesswoman of the Year. When she set up her first Body Shop Anita couldn't afford smart containers to put her products in – which is why many Body Shop lotions were sold in bottles more usually used for urine samples.

And did you know that . . .
The largest solid gold object in existence is King Tutankhamen's coffin, weighing 2,450lb?
There are estimated to be 16 million thunderstorms throughout the world each year?

NOTES

On Japan...

I was a soldier in Japan 35 years ago – I spent my time in camp training for Korea. I never saw a Japanese man wearing a suit; it felt like three hundred years ago when I was there.   (10 March)

MARCH 1988

14 MONDAY

Albert Einstein, the world's greatest physicist, was born today in 1879. He will always be remembered for his work which enabled the creation of the first atomic bomb, but when he heard about the annihilation of Hiroshima he said, 'Had I known, I would have become a plumber.'

And did you know that . . .
The thighbone is the strongest bone in the body and can support more pressure than a solid steel rod of the same size?

15 TUESDAY

A young Yugoslavian husband played a practical joke on his wife three years ago today. He came home wearing a horror mask, then prowled outside the house, occasionally knocking on the door. His poor wife was so terrified by the masked intruder that she took a shotgun and blasted him dead.

And did you know that . . .
The Queen's dogs dine on fresh rabbit, pork and chicken and very rarely on tinned food?

16 WEDNESDAY

A postal sorting office on the outskirts of Paris was brought to a halt today in 1980 when one of the workers noticed that a package was humming. The place was cleared and the bomb squad brought in. They gingerly opened the parcel – and found a vibrator that had switched itself on.

And did you know that . . .
There are around 4,000 different recognized types of knot?
*   It takes about six years to grow hair long enough to sit on?*
*   Indian eunuchs have the support of the Delhi Eunuch Welfare Society?*

17 THURSDAY

Patrick Duffy, better known as *Dallas*'s Bobby Ewing, is 39 today. When Bobby was killed off the ratings slumped, so the producers looked around to a way of raising him from the dead. A mysterious twin brother? A ghost? No – they simply pretended that his death, and everything that had happened in the intervening months, was a bad dream.

And did you know that . . .
The blood of insects is almost colourless?

MARCH 1988

18 FRIDAY

After several years living side by side in Washington Zoo, giant pandas Hsing-Hsing and Ling-Ling finally found themselves in the mood for love today in 1983.

And did you know that . . .

Historians have calculated that over the last 3,500 years there have been only 230 years of peace in the civilized world?

Roy Rogers's famous horse and dog have been stuffed and put on display in the Roy Rogers Museum?

The most common surname in China is Chang?

19 SATURDAY

Ursula Andress, the best Bond girl of them all, is 52 today. She has the distinction of being one of the first actresses to take part in official nude screen tests, held for the 1963 movie *Four for Texas*. Such care with casting wasn't necessary as things turned out. The censor cut all the nude scenes.

And did you know that . . .

A 10-gallon hat only holds around ¾ of a gallon?

British women buy almost twice as many pairs of men's underpants as men do?

20 SUNDAY

Today in 1980 Radio Caroline, the pirate station that revolutionized the airwaves in the sixties, sank in a stormy sea off Kent. Many famous DJs served their apprenticeship at sea on the *Mi Amigo*, the station's home. Among them are Tony Blackburn, Emperor Rosko and Dave Lee Travis.

And did you know that . . .

Flamingos can only eat with their heads held upside down?

Only male canaries can sing?

If goldfish are left in a darkened room for a long time they go silver?

NOTES

_____

_____

_____

_____

MARCH 1988

21 MONDAY

Timothy Dalton, the latest James Bond, is 42 today. Ian Fleming, the man who invented 007, once boasted that he wrote for 'warm-blooded heterosexuals in railway trains, aeroplanes and bed'. Judging from his enormous success, there are a lot of warm-blooded heterosexuals out there.

And did you know that . . .

In the USA it is a criminal offence to alter the tune of 'The Star-Spangled Banner?
 St Matthew is the patron saint of accountants?

22 TUESDAY

Today's the day that Chico Marx was born in 1891. Chico had two great interests in life – gambling and women. One day his wife caught him kissing a chorus girl. 'I wasn't kissing her,' he protested, 'I was just whispering in her mouth.'

And did you know that . . .

There are half a million John Smiths living in the USA?
 The first seven presidents of the USA were not US citizens?

23 WEDNESDAY

Nothing is quite as it seems, as the residents of Wood Green in north London discovered 70 years ago tonight. The magician Chung Ling Soo was killed while performing his famous act – catching in his teeth bullets fired from a rifle. Not only did it turn out that the gun was a fake; *he* was a fake too. Chung Ling Soo was none other than plain Bill Robinson from New York.

And did you know that . . .

In 1978 James Dean's signature sold for twice as much as Abraham Lincoln's?
 Two out of five American women dye their hair?

24 THURSDAY

55 years ago today polythene was discovered by accident. There was just one problem when it came to manufacturing large amounts of the substance – the factories tended to explode if they weren't shut down once in a while.

And did you know that . . .

Each morning Britain's men shave off 159,000 miles of beard?
 In New York you can dial a telephone gardener to talk to your plants?

MARCH 1988

25 FRIDAY

Five years ago the townspeople of Legnano, birthplace of composer Antonio Salieri, decided to hit back at the attack made on him in the Oscar-winning film *Amadeus*. They voted to erect a statue to him and hold a convention to clear him of the charge of murdering Mozart.

And did you know that . . .

New York City has more rain in the average year than London?
The inhabitants of ancient Carthage rubbed a cow's tail on their stomachs to cure indigestion?

26 SATURDAY

Prince William shook the hand of the pilot who flew him from Aberdeen to London today in 1985. He was two years old and it was his first public handshake – the first of many.

And did you know that . . .

If all the eggs laid by hens in the USA every year were laid end to end they would encircle the Earth a hundred times?
Two million pigs are turned into Spam each year?

27 SUNDAY

English author Arnold Bennett died today in 1931. He was a great expert on death and boasted that every detail of Darius Clayhanger's last gasps in his *Clayhanger* series was researched in detail. 'I took infinite pains over it,' he boasted. 'All the time my father was dying I was at the bedside making copious notes.'

And did you know that . . .

The table fork was introduced to England by Thomas Coryat in 1608?
Chihuahua dogs were originally bred for their meat?

NOTES

On Music...

I have the most eclectic appreciation of music – I go right from Mozart and Mahler to Madonna. I know what the Top 20 is at any given moment, which makes me popular with my daughters. I'm totally and utterly fascinated by music – and cannot play a single instrument!

(25 March)

MARCH 1988

28
MONDAY

Five years ago today reports came in from Berlin that a vagrant had been discovered cooking soup on the 'eternal flame' – which is intended to burn until the two parts of Germany are reunited. It was his second offence; the first time he'd been caught trying to make dumplings.

And did you know that . . .

More than twice as many cars as babies are made each year in the USA?

   The inhabitants of Korea eat around 30,000 snakes each day?
   The study of beauty is called kalology?

29
TUESDAY

102 years ago today the very first Coca-Cola was brewed and sold as 'Esteemed Brain Tonic and Intellectual Beverage'. It was supposed to help against headaches and hangovers and it may well have been effective since its chief ingredient was the leaves of the coca plant – the main source of cocaine.

And did you know that . . .

The earliest recorded English horse race was held at Netherby in Yorkshire in AD210?

   A survey has shown that 24 per cent of marriage proposals in the USA are made in cars?

30
WEDNESDAY

Two years ago one of Hollywood's most enduring partnerships was ended when James Cagney died. He and his wife Frances, who was once his professional dancing partner, had been married an amazing 63 years.

And did you know that . . .

When you get up in the morning you are about 6mm taller than you were when you went to bed the night before?

31
THURSDAY

The Clasp Locker or Unlocker for Shoes was patented 95 years ago today and revolutionized the world under its popular name – the zip. Whitcomb L. Judson was the man who got the credit for it but in fact it was Elias Howe, the man who invented the first sewing machine, who'd actually dreamed up the idea.

And did you know that . . .

The Earth's rotation is gradually slowing and we will eventually have another day each year?

APRIL 1988

1 FRIDAY

The seafront at Brighton was crowded eight years ago today – not with sunbathers but with people trying to spot a nudist. For the first time skinny-dippers could legally bare their all on Brighton beach, but unfortunately it was so cold and wet that few of them braved the weather and the audience.

And did you know that . . .
In the USA there's a magazine called Chocolate News*? It comes in a glossy brown cover and actually smells of chocolate.*

2 SATURDAY

The first human cannonball was a woman, and she was fired for the first time today in 1877 at Westminster. Her 60-foot flight caused such a sensation that she made a career of it, earned a fortune and died 50 years later of natural causes.

And did you know that . . .
Paul Roget, who compiled the famous Thesaurus, also invented the slide rule?

3 SUNDAY

Two years ago today peace was declared after a war that no one had noticed for 335 years. In 1651 the Dutch launched an attack on the Scilly Isles in an attempt to capture the pirates who operated there. The Scilly Islanders refused to surrender and Admiral Tromp declared war on them. Then the English stepped in, the war was forgotten – and so was the peace treaty.

And did you know that . . .
In America there are towns named Bacon (Georgia), Cocoa (Florida), Intercourse (Pennsylvania) and Truth or Consequence (New Mexico)?

NOTES

1 April: *Good Friday — Public holiday in Great Britain and Northern Ireland.*
3 April: *Easter Day.*

On Useful Inventions...

I heard they've never definitely found the guy who actually invented the safety-pin — I'm just trying to figure out a way of getting the royalties and rights for all the safety pins ever sold!

(31 March)

APRIL 1988

4
MONDAY

A report published four years ago today described how a New Zealand man had beaten his wife to death with a frozen sausage.

And did you know that . . .
20,000 men died while building the Panama Canal?
    The oldest continually inhabited city in the Americas is Cuzco, the ancient Inca capital of Peru?
    Rainbows can be seen on moonlit showery nights?

5
TUESDAY

65 years ago today Lord Carnarvon died – the first victim of Tutankhamen's curse. His death was put down to a mosquito bite, which was noted to be in the same position as a blemish on the mummified body of the boy king. Seven years later only two of the original team who had discovered the tomb were still alive.

And did you know that . . .

Kapok, used for stuffing cushions and mattresses, grows on trees?

6
WEDNESDAY

News came in from Florida two years ago today that a man who had been charged with kidnapping a girl was later charged with theft. It emerged that he thought he was a vampire and had drunk, and thus stolen, her blood.

And did you know that . . .
Soldiers in the West German army have been issued with hairnets?
    An American man has successfully breastfed his baby after a course of hormone tablets?
    Israeli cows are issued with identity cards?

7
THURSDAY

William Wordsworth was born today in 1770. For many years he lived at Grasmere in the Lake District with his sister and walked the area taking notes and composing his poems. He was at one time thought to be a French spy and was followed for a whole month by a detective.

And did you know that . . .
There are 4,500 symbols in the Chinese alphabet?
    There is a small fish known to Hawaiians as homomomonukunukuaguk?
    Hail falls most frequently in June?

APRIL 1988

8 FRIDAY

Clint Eastwood was voted Mayor of Carmel, California, two years ago today. There was no suggestion that he stood for office because of the salary that went with the title. It was only £133 a month.

And did you know that . . .

The deepest lake in the world is Lake Baykal in Russia, which is at some points a mile deep?

9 SATURDAY

The World's Sweetheart was born today in 1894. Mary Pickford's childlike innocence made her the most popular movie actress in the world for many years, but beneath that simpering look she was a tough business lady. A founder of the United Artists studio, she was one of the richest women in America. As Samuel Goldwyn said, 'It took longer to make one of Mary's contracts than it did to make one of Mary's pictures.'

And did you know that . . .

There are 156 languages in the world that are spoken by at least one million people?

10 SUNDAY

The world's skinniest man was born today in 1797. Claude Seurat was so thin that when he exhibited himself in London in 1825 people queued round the block to take a look at him. His biceps measured just four inches round and the back-to-chest thickness of his body was just three inches.

And did you know that . . .

John F. Kennedy was suffering from a form of leukaemia when he was killed?

Edison and Einstein were both failures at school?

There have been 60 filmed versions of Hamlet*?*

NOTES

4 April: *Easter Monday — Public holiday in Great Britain and Northern Ireland.*

On *Hamlet . . .*

My one brush with the Bard was in a TV film of *Hamlet.* **I played Horatio to Christopher Plummer's prince and the play was shot on location at Elsinore Castle – a romantic location, except for the twentieth-century foghorn which kept booming every fifteen minutes. Instead of filming long scenes the whole thing had to be done in ten-minute takes!** (10 April)

APRIL 1988

11 MONDAY

Four years ago today a Glasgow couple put their old electric table lamp up for auction at Christie's and got £421,200 for it. The base of the lamp was a fourteenth-century Chinese porcelain vase that they'd never got round to throwing away.

And did you know that . . .

The Mercedes car is named after Mercedes Jellinck, daughter of a director of the Daimler company?

Christmas cards were first engraved by an American company?

12 TUESDAY

Two years ago *The Times* carried news of a new form of marine life discovered by biologists working off Australia and New Zealand. Christened the Sea Daisy because of its shape, it has no stomach, stores food in its feet and has ten sex organs.

And did you know that . . .

Mediaeval monks used to call the toilet the necessarium?

More than 20 million Americans can play the piano?

The first American bank was robbed in 1883?

13 WEDNESDAY

Samuel Beckett is 82 today. He's renowned for his plays that comment on the desolate condition of society and also for asking the actors and actresses who perform them to do almost impossible things – from sitting in dustbins to being buried up to their necks in earth.

And did you know that . . .

During the reign of William the Conqueror, hunting hounds which did not belong to the king had to have three toes chopped off to slow them down and prevent them from catching game?

14 THURSDAY

66 years ago there was a terrible night to remember when the *Titanic*, the unsinkable ship, hit an iceberg and went down with 1,500 passengers. 14 years before the tragedy, Morgan Robertson wrote a novel called *The Wreck of the Titan* about the maiden voyage of a fictional luxury liner which was sunk by an iceberg on a foggy April night. Even more of a coincidence, Robertson's fictional ship had far too few lifeboats to save all the passengers – just like the *Titanic*.

APRIL 1988

Tommy Cooper, the nation's much-loved worst magician, died on stage during a television broadcast two years ago. He started as a straight performer but after one terrible night when every trick went wrong he realized that the audience was laughing even more than usual. After that he didn't even try to make his magic work.

And did you know that . . .
In the USA more soft drinks are consumed each day than any other kind of liquid – including tea, coffee or even tapwater?

Charlie Chaplin was born today in 1889. He once entered a Charlie Chaplin look-alike competition in Monte Carlo and came third.

And did you know that . . .
There's no lead in modern lead pencils?
*   According to researchers at Brigham Young University, more than 15 per cent of Americans bite their toenails?*
*   An emu once removed the hearing aid of a visitor to London Zoo and swallowed it?*

Two years ago the Chinese launched an anti-smoking campaign and used as a cautionary example the case of a two-year-old baby who smokes around four cigarettes a day and cries if he's refused a light.

And did you know that . . .
When you stroke a dog or cat your blood pressure drops – and so does the animal's?
*   It's possible to transplant fingernails?*
*   A 1972 survey revealed that more than 14 per cent of Italian prostitutes have university degrees?*

NOTES

On Impersonation...

I have trouble with impersonators like Charlie Chaplin did. I was watching TV one day and an advert for cigars came on, with the Invisible Man wearing a pair of glasses and talking in this strange voice. I associate the Invisible Man with Claude Rains, who had a beautiful voice. 'Why have they got this bloody awful voice with the Invisible Man?' I asked my wife. She said, 'It's yours!' 'I don't talk like that,' I said. 'Oh yes you do,' she told me. I've never done a commercial, and for people to think that I had... I didn't like that and they took the advert off altogether.

(16 April)

APRIL 1988

18
MONDAY

The San Francisco earthquake struck 80 years ago today, killing more than 500 people and doing around $500 million worth of damage. Among the people caught in the chaos was the tenor Enrico Caruso who fled into the streets clutching a picture of Teddy Roosevelt. He swore later that he would never go back to a city 'where disorders like that are permitted.'

And did you know that . . .
An explosion in a munitions factory in Stockholm was discovered to have been caused by a spark from a female worker's underwear?
*   Spinach contains no more iron than any other vegetable?*

19
TUESDAY

Lord Byron, sex-mad Romantic poet, died today in 1824. He was the proud owner of a Newfoundland dog called Bos'un at a time when Newfoundlands were all the rage. They were famous for their lifesaving achievements and at one point a number of them were stationed as lifeguards along the Seine, in Paris. Unfortunately the plan had to be dropped after one particularly careful dog kept pulling swimmers out whether they were in trouble or not.

And did you know that . . .
When you blush, the lining of your stomach turns red too – and it turns pale when you do?

20
WEDNESDAY

99 years ago today Adolf Hitler was born. He grew up to be a vegetarian and an animal lover who taught his pet Alsatian to do tricks. He was also said to have only one testicle and is believed by some to have died a virgin despite his mistresses and marriage to Eva Braun.

And did you know that . . .
Marie Antoinette wore potato flowers in her hat to promote the popularity of the vegetable?
*   A group of bears is known as a 'sleuth'?*

21
THURSDAY

The Queen is 62 today! This is her real birthday, not her official one which occurs in June. Maybe she'll have a banquet to celebrate. If she does, the place settings will be precisely measured with a ruler and the waiters will work in perfect unison, directed by a set of red and green cue lights discreetly hidden behind the throne.

APRIL 1988

22
FRIDAY

The passionate reputation of Italians was boosted two years ago when a council official in Naples suggested creating a special park in which people could make love in their cars without fear of being spied on by Peeping Toms.

23
SATURDAY

Remember blonde mop-top movie star Shirley Temple? Believe it or not, she's 60 today. Before she was 10 she was the darling of the world with fans including Princess Elizabeth and Franklin D. Roosevelt, who wrote to her frequently. Once, when it was reported that she had been taken ill, 20,000 Balinese islanders got together to pray for her recovery.

And did you know that . . .

The expression 'mad as a hatter' derives from the time when hatmakers used mercury on felt hats? They were slowly poisoned, and the effect of mercury poisoning made them seem mad and eccentric?

24
SUNDAY

A 16-year-old public schoolboy was crowned King Makhosetive of Swaziland two years ago today. The new king, who selected his first wife from among thousands of bare-breasted beauties when he was only 14, was sent to school at Sherborne, Dorset, as a way of keeping him safe from tribal rivalries. The plan didn't work. In 1984 an African witch-doctor carrying a poisonous potion was found in Dorset, looking for him.

And did you know that . . .

The Tour d'Argent *restaurant in Paris is famed for its dish of pressed duck served in its own juices? Every customer who orders the speciality is presented with an individually-numbered card which records their visit. Charlie Chaplin ate duck number 253,652.*

NOTES

On Working with Children and Animals . . .

I've worked with kids in films and I don't mind them. They don't steal scenes from adults, what happens is they cock them up. It's the same with animals. You have to do a scene over and over again until the kid or the animal gets it right, then they print that take. It's usually the one where *you're* caught picking your nose!

(23 April)

APRIL 1988

25
MONDAY

Today in 1926 Reza Shah took his place on the Peacock throne of Persia after staging an armed coup. Although he was the son of a peasant, he took to absolute power as if he had been born to it. When visiting the outlying parts of his country he travelled in an armour-plated Rolls Royce and when he stayed the night in a village all the local dogs were slaughtered in case their barking woke him.

And did you know that . . .
   The most popular British dog's name in 1986 was Ben?

26
TUESDAY

The Tiller Girls, founded by John Tiller in 1886, celebrate 102 years of high-kicking today.

And did you know that . . .
Among sweet foods, doughnuts are one of the least harmful to the teeth?
   Peter the Great of Russia disliked beards so much that he once decreed that all bearded men should be shaved by force with a blunt razor?

27
WEDNESDAY

Samuel Morse, inventor of the Morse code, was born today in 1791. He was an artist by training and served as the first President of the National School of Design in the USA before deciding at the age of 40 to start work on the telegraph system.

And did you know that . . .
The Canary Island are not named after birds but dogs? The original name for the islands was Insulae Canariae, *meaning 'Islands of the Dogs'.*

28
THURSDAY

41 years ago today adventurer Thor Heyerdahl set out from Peru on a 4,300-mile journey to the South Seas. His craft was the *Kon-Tiki*, a raft made of balsa wood and rope which he had constructed in an attempt to prove that early explorers could have made the trip.

And did you know that . . .
More perfume is used in Russia than in any other country?
   Mrs Marva Drew of Iowa took five years to type all the numbers from 1 to 1,000,000 after her son's teacher said it wasn't possible?

APRIL 1988

29 FRIDAY

Sir Thomas Beecham, famous conductor and wit, was born today in 1879. He was rehearsing with an orchestra one day and things were not going well – some of the players weren't keeping time. Beecham turned to one of the worst offenders with the words, 'We cannot expect you to be with us the whole time, but maybe you would be kind enough to keep in touch now and again?'

And did you know that . . .
All polar bears are left-handed?

30 SATURDAY

43 years ago today Hitler committed suicide in his bunker under the Chancellory in Berlin. He shot himself and Evan Braun took a cyanide capsule. The day before they had tested the capsules by giving one to Blondi, Hitler's Alsatian. It had worked.

And did you know that . . .
Dogs, cats, rats and mice all have a bone in their penis?
*   Around nine hundred different chemicals are contained in cigarette smoke?*

NOTES

_____
_____
_____
_____
_____
_____

THINGS TO DO IN MAY:

_____
_____
_____
_____
_____

MAY 1988

1
SUNDAY

76 years ago today the famous statue of Peter Pan was erected in Kensington Gardens. In the original version of J.M. Barrie's play, Peter told the Darling children that they would be able to fly if only they *believed* they could. Several children who'd seen the play were injured when they tried this out for themselves, so Barrie hastily inserted another vital ingredient – fairy dust.

And did you know that . . .
The largest accurately-measured iceberg was larger than Belgium?

NOTES

_____

_____

_____

_____

_____

MAY 1988

2
MONDAY

Leonardo da Vinci died today in 1519. His most famous work, the *Mona Lisa*, was stolen from the Louvre in 1911 by Vincenzo Peruggia who kept it in a trunk under his bed for two years.

And did you know that . . .

A Los Angeles woman has had her Pekingese dog freeze-dried and now keeps him on a coffee table in her lounge?

To achieve her famous cheekbones, Marlene Dietrich had her back teeth removed?

3
TUESDAY

90 years ago Golda Meir, Prime Minister of Israel, was born in Russia. She was one of the first women to achieve high political office; when asked what it felt like to be the first woman foreign minister Mrs Meir said simply, 'I don't know. I was never a man minister.'

And did you know that . . .

A 1978 survey in France revealed that 54 per cent of adults had not read a book from cover to cover since they had left school?

4
WEDNESDAY

One year ago today modern disco-style dancing was given the go-ahead in China on the following conditions: i) The lights must be bright; ii) the bands must wear smart matching jackets or uniforms; iii) no alcohol is served; iv) only officially-approved music is to be played; and v) each band must be able to play at least two different tunes.

And did you know that . . .

The first advert on Radio Luxembourg was for a laxative?

Around 6 million South Koreans have the surname Kim?

The Zonda, the Oe and the Elephanta are all types of wind?

5
THURSDAY

The first instalment of the eagerly-awaited Hitler diaries was published in *Stern* magazine this week in 1983. Despite experts' doubts about their authenticity, *Stern* had spent £2.5 million on the set of notebooks marked TOP SECRET, PROPERTY OF THE FUHRER. Just five days after the first revelations it was discovered that they were definitely fakes; they'd been written by an East German railway porter.

And did you know that . . .

In Kentucky it used to be illegal for a man to purchase a hat without his wife in attendance?

MAY 1988

6 FRIDAY

34 years ago today Roger Bannister ran the world's first sub-four-minute mile. In charge of recording the time – 3 minutes 59.4 seconds – was Norris McWhirter, one of the founders of the *Guinness Book of Records.*

And did you know that . . .
Rin Tin Tin was voted the Most Popular Film Performer of 1926, beating Charlie Chaplin and Rudolph Valentino.

7 SATURDAY

Evan Perón, Argentinian cult figure, was born today in 1919. After her death in 1952 her body was embalmed and laid in state. Three years later, after a military coup, her remains were taken to Italy and buried, then exhumed and taken to Madrid. Finally in 1976 she was flown back to Argentina and interred for the last time.

And did you know that . . .
The British eat more sweets and confectionary than any other nation does?

8 SUNDAY

Today, and on this date every year, the residents of Helston don their finery and skip through the streets in the Furry Dance. According to legend the Devil once flew across Cornwall carrying a boulder and was challenged by St Michael. In the battle that followed the Devil dropped his burden, and the place where it fell became known as Hell's Stone – or Helston. Since then the locals have celebrated the triumph of good over evil with their famous dance.

And did you know that . . .
Chess is the most widely played game in Russia?

NOTES

2 May: *Public holiday in UK.*

On *Mona Lisa* **...**

I did *Mona Lisa* **as a favour to Neil Jordan and Bob Hoskins. It was something I did to encourage another British movie and to get some notice for an actor I admire tremendously and a director who I think is going to be a big name. It's a good film, and funnily enough the** *Mona Lisa* **production offices were in the hospital where I was born. St Olave's in Rotherhithe has been converted into offices, so I'm the first actor in history to make a film from the hospital where he was born!** (2 May)

MAY 1988

9 MONDAY

Today is Mr Punch's official 326th birthday. Not many people know that until 1818 Punch's partner was called Joan and that Toby was traditionally a real dog. And during the Crimean War the crocodile was for a while replaced by the Russian Bear as a symbol of evil.

And did you know that . . .

Early condoms were made from linen fabric soaked in chemicals?
  Georges Simenon, who created Maigret, claims to have slept with 10,000 women?

10 TUESDAY

Dancing star Fred Astaire was born today in 1899. He was born Frederick Austerlitz and, accoridng to Graham Greene, his immense popularity was based on the fact that he's 'The nearest we are ever likely to get to a human Mickey Mouse.'

And did you know that . . .

During the final years of the reign of George III, who suffered from an illness that made him appear mad, performances of King Lear, *Shakespeare's play about a mad king, were banned?*

11 WEDNESDAY

Five years ago it was officially declared that there were more kangaroos (19 million) in Australia than people (15 million).

And did you know that . . .

Kangaroos can't jump if their tails are lifted off the ground?
  The Turkish Van Cat loves swimming?
  Spencer Tracy was once awarded an Oscar with the inscription addressed to Dick Tracy?
  Xylophones are usually made of rosewood?

12 THURSDAY

Today in 1820 Florence Nightingale was born. She was named after the city of her birth. Her sister, who was born while their globe-trotting parents were in Greece, was named Parthenope.

And did you know that . . .

People who live in the country stand further apart from each other at parties than people used to crowded town life?
  Safeway is the world's largest supermarket chain?
  Cats cannot taste sweet things?

MAY 1988

13 FRIDAY

Sir Arthur Sullivan, the composing half of the great Gilbert and Sullivan partnership, was born today in 1842. He and W.S. Gilbert did not get on well together and on three occasions they swore never to work with each other again. From 1871 to 1896 most of their collaborative work was conducted via the post.

And did you know that . . .
People from large cities walk faster than people who live in the country?
  Nine out of ten people are right-handed?

14 SATURDAY

According to a Labour report on the EEC published five years ago, the following amount of fruit had been destroyed or dumped each hour of the previous year: 5,266 oranges, 1,579 peaches and 134lb of apples.

And did you know that . . .
The average age of air stewardesses is rising? 20 years ago most stewardesses were in their early 20s; today the average age is around 30.
  Gorillas have hair all over their bodies, except for their chests?

15 SUNDAY

48 years ago today the world's first nylon stockings were put on sale. They were a great success; 72,000 pairs were sold in New York in just one day.

And did you know that . . .
In 1924 a tourist was talked into 'buying' Big Ben for £1,000?
  It's estimated that each year tourists visiting the Great Pyramid take about a ton of it home with them, in the form of souvenirs?
  A snake in Philadelphia Zoo bit itself to death? Whether it was an accident or suicide no one could say.

NOTES

On the Oscars...

Naturally it was tremendous to receive an Oscar for *Hannah and Her Sisters*. Afterwards people asked Woody Allen why he'd chosen me for the film and not Marlon Brando or someone like that – even *I* didn't think I was the Woody Allen type. He said, 'There are very few actors like Michael. He has vulnerability. He always looks as if he could be hurt. Most movie stars don't.'

(11 May)

MAY 1988

16
MONDAY

Three years ago the Mexican one-peso coin was scrapped after complaints from vending machine owners in the USA that it was exactly the same shape and size as a 25-cent piece but worth 50 times less.

And did you know that . . .

In the late 1970s more bicycles were made in the USA each year than cars?

In 1968, 1 in every 32 British postmen was bitten by a dog?

17
TUESDAY

Spitting was outlawed in Peking today in 1985. The Chinese authorities established 147,000 inspectors with the power to fine offenders 14p on the spot and give them a lecture on the disgusting nature of their habit.

And did you know that . . .

In 56 days the silkworm can eat 86,000 times its own weight?

There is a Harrods in Buenos Aires?

Paul Revere was the first person to advertise false teeth for sale in the USA?

18
WEDNESDAY

At 8.32 a.m. eight years ago today Mount St Helens blew up with a force equivalent to 500 of the atomic bombs dropped on Hiroshima. 400 million tons of ash and debris were blasted into the atmosphere and formed a cloud 2,500 miles long and 1,000 miles wide.

And did you know that . . .

A Norwich Zoo flamingo was fitted with a false leg after breaking its own?

President Reagan once bought a baby elephant from Harrods?

19
THURSDAY

One year ago today a hundred cats were put on display in the first official Russian cat show. Dogs are more popular pets in Russia than cats.

And did you know that . . .

A survey in America revealed that the average family throws away about 10 per cent of the food it buys?

Caterpillars have 2,000 muscles; man has only 650?

Research shows that elderly people are less likely to die in the two months before their birthday than in the two months afterwards?

MAY 1988

20 FRIDAY

Dentists were working in the Negev desert 2,500 years ago. That was the finding of a team of Israeli archaeologists three years ago today when they discovered a skeleton that had had root canal work done on its teeth.

And did you know that . . .

Four out of ten children claim to have watched video nasties?
*   The first Ferris wheel, invented by George Ferris, was erected in 1893?*
*   Most snowflakes are hexagonal?*
*   The tallest bamboo in the world reaches heights of 120 feet?*

21 SATURDAY

61 years ago today Charles Lindburgh completed his solo New York–Paris non-stop flight. He took no parachute and had the windows taken out of his plane, *The Spirit of St Louis*, in an attempt to cut down on the weight.

And did you know that . . .

There was an attempt in California to introduce a law exempting drivers with no hands from having to pay for the use of parking meters?
*   The word 'shampoo' comes from the Hindi word 'to press'?*
*   Julio Inglesias used to play for Real Madrid football team?*
*   Several hundred new species of insect are discovered each year?*

22 SUNDAY

According to a survey published three years ago today, three million Britons are either vegetarian or have cut red meat from their diet.

And did you know that . . .

The Mediterranean is the most polluted sea in the world?
*   The world's first machine gun fired square bullets?*
*   Proportionally speaking, if humans could jump as high as fleas they would be able to leap over St Paul's Cathedral?*
*   The umbrella was invented by the ancient Egptians?*

NOTES

_____

_____

_____

MAY 1988

23 MONDAY

Joan Collins is 55 today. Exactly a year after she was born Bonnie and Clyde were gunned down in Louisiana. Bonnie was shot 55 times, Clyde 27.

And did you know that . . .

Many species of oyster change their sex around four times a year?

The Greek dramatist Aeschylus was killed when a tortoise fell on his head?

The Earth hurtles through space at 66,620 mph?

Tarantulas don't spin webs?

Roller skates were invented as an aid to health?

24 TUESDAY

Today in 1974 the great Duke Ellington died in a New York hospital. Just the day before the *Bath and West Evening Chronicle* had featured an article about him which began with the words, 'Bandleaders come and go, but the perennial Duke Ellington, like Tennyson's brook, seems to go on for ever.'

And did you know that . . .

Until the late 1940s it was forbidden to mention commercial travellers, honeymoon couples, lodgers and phrases such as 'winter draws on' on BBC radio?

The silk-worm moth has 11 brains?

25 WEDNESDAY

Three years ago Lynne Frederick, widow of Peter Sellers, was awarded $1 million damages over *The Trail of the Pink Panther* – the first film to be 'made' after the death of its star and consisting of scenes edited from his earlier movies.

And did you know that . . .

The average lifespan for a caveman was 18 years and for ancient Romans 22 years?

26 THURSDAY

George Formby was born 84 years ago today. His father wanted him to be a jockey but he took up the ukelele and became one of the world's most unlikely film stars. The ukelele originally came from Portugal and its name means 'jumping flea'.

And did you know that . . .

Utopia officially exists – on Mars?

MAY 1988

27 FRIDAY

Today is a good day for horror fans. Christopher Lee and Vincent Price were both born today, Lee in 1922 and Price in 1911. Both have played Dracula, but only once has the vampire Count been portrayed as described in Bram Stoker's novel – with a moustache.

And did you know that . . .

In Vienna there is a cinema that shows nothing but James Bond films?

A whale's heart beats only 540 times an hour?

28 SATURDAY

William Pitt the Younger was born today in 1759. Records show he was a hard drinker. He disposed of 2,410 bottles of port, 854 bottles of Madeira and 574 bottles of claret in one year and his reported last words on his deathbed were, 'I think I could eat one of Bellamy's veal pies.'

And did you know that . . .

King Louis XVI of France loved chocolate so much that he appointed a court official, the Chocolatier to the King, to be in charge of it?

29 SUNDAY

35 years ago today Sir Edmund Hillary and Sherpa Tenzing became the first men to reach the summit of Mount Everest. There is a distance of more than 12 miles between the highest and lowest points of the earth. Everest rises more than 29,000 feet; the Mariana Trench in the Pacific Ocean reaches 36,000 below sea level.

A French magazine which conducted a poll into the national sex life discovered that the average French man admitted to sleeping with 11.8 women while French women admitted to sleeping with only 1.8 men.

NOTES

23 May: *Public holiday in UK.*

On Peter Sellers...

Peter Sellers and I were great friends. He had a reputation for being a difficult man; the problem was that he never came out of the same box twice – you couldn't anticipate how he was going to be. Not many people know that he really wanted to be a Cockney. In fact he was a closet Cockney. There are things about his humour that most people don't understand, except Cockneys!

(25 May)

MAY 1988

MONDAY

Joan of Arc was burnt at the stake 557 years ago today. She was not born in France, as most people think, but in the independent Duchy of Lorraine which did not officially become part of the French Kingdom until 1776.

And did you know that . . .

A survey in the USA reveals that at times of national stress, like wars and recessions, people chew more chewing gum?

Louis XIV used to grant audiences while he was sitting on the loo?

Sturgeon mate for life?

TUESDAY

60 years ago today the last Model T Ford was produced. In 1908 preparations for the car brought Henry Ford so close to bankruptcy that he had to borrow $100 from a friend's sister to pay for its launch. Ten years later Ford was a millionaire and the generous lady received more than $250,000 for her loan.

And did you know that . . .

The Duke of Wellington invented a walking stick with an ear trumpet in its handle?

The Berlin Wall displays the longest stretch of grafitti in the world?

The muffin is the official food symbol of Massachusetts?

NOTES

On Cars . . .

My first car was a Rolls Royce; a black Rolls Royce. Black goes with everything. The day I bought it I jotted it down on a shopping list – a packet of razor blades, a loaf of bread, 1lb of butter, cornflakes and a Rolls Royce!

(31 May)

THINGS TO DO IN JUNE:

JUNE 1988

1 WEDNESDAY

Marilyn Monroe was born 62 years ago today. Her secret ambition was to make a film of Dostoevsky's *Brothers Karamazov*, but no one took her seriously. When she married respected playwright Arthur Miller the headlines declared EGGHEAD MARRIES HOURGLASS.

And did you know that . . .

The beefalo is a cross between a buffalo and an ordinary beef breed?

Goats never close their eyes when they sleep? They only doze and the slightest sound wakes them up.

Antarctica is the highest, coldest, stormiest and driest continent on Earth?

The first elephant twins on record were born in Tanzania in 1976?

The French town of Cognac holds an annual festival of detective films?

Queen Victoria was once given a musical bustle?

You can be fined for walking more than two abreast in the narrow streets of Toledo?

King Sepor II of Persia was crowned before he was born?

2 THURSDAY

Two years ago Yoshi Kamata, famous for being the oldest woman in Japan, had a nasty shock. It was discovered that 10 years had been added to her age and that instead of being 110 she was only 100.

And did you know that . . .

The bat is the only genuine flying mammal?

Catalan is the official language of Andorra?

To compensate for the effects of the high altitude, Andean Indians have larger lungs and more blood than average?

The bootlace worm, usually found in the North Sea, can be as much as 180 feet long?

King James I of England was the first British monarch to use a fork?

Grace Kelly, the late Princess Grace of Monaco, was the first Hollywood movie star to appear on a postage stamp?

Butterflies taste things with their back feet?

The World Championship Armadillo races are held in Texas every October?

It is illegal to kick a mule in Arizona?

A seven-year-old girl passed tests designed for adults to become a member of MENSA?

Llama, camel and horse milk are widely drunk around the world?

JUNE 1988

3 FRIDAY

Two years ago today American researchers published a survey of sex and single women in their twenties. It was discovered that four out of five had had sex; one third had been pregnant at least once; and on average each single woman in her twenties had had 4.5 lovers.

And did you know that . . .
Crete, New Zealand, Iceland and Malta have no native snakes?
  During the seven years he was poet laureate William Wordsworth did not write a single poem?

4 SATURDAY

75 years ago Suffragette Emily Wilding Davison stepped out in front of the King's horse, Anmer, as it thundered round Tattenham Corner in the Derby, and was killed. She was not immediately recognized as a martyr for her cause; *The Times* was more concerned with the fact that she might have injured the horse.

And did you know that . . .
John Dillinger robbed more banks in one year than Jesse James did in 16 years?

5 SUNDAY

The Arab-Israeli Six-Day War started 21 years ago today when Nasser, with the backing of Syria and Jordan, ordered the UN peace-keeping force out of the Sinai buffer-zone. Six days later it was all over. The Israelis struck with such speed that most of the Egyptian planes were destroyed while they were still on the ground.

And did you know that . . .
The phrase 'the real McCoy' originated with rumrunner Bill McCoy? His rum was simply the best, so people used to ask for 'the real McCoy'.
  The tench hibernates for the winter in the mud on the bottom of lakes?

NOTES

On Sex and the Single Woman...

I think Brigitte Bardot was the first truly liberated woman. I met her in Spain, years ago when she was very young and just having fun. She had fun like a guy; she used to pick up any man who caught her eye!
(3 June)

JUNE 1988

6 MONDAY

John Paul Getty, the richest private citizen in the world, died today in 1976. The Getty Museum, which he founded and funded, is now the envy of other museums around the world; it is legally forced to spend $1.5 million a week on acquisitions.

And did you know that . . .
A blue whale is so large than an African elephant could fit on its tongue?
70 per cent of ordinary house dust consists of shed skin particles?

7 TUESDAY

25 years ago today the Rolling Stones made their first TV appearance on 'Thank Your Lucky Stars'. Not everyone was convinced of their star quality. One TV producer watched them and then advised their manager to get rid of the singer 'with the tyre-tread lips'.

And did you know that . . .
The Chinese were the first to record the tug-of-war as a sport?
The bald eagle is not bald?
The liver of the polar bear is so rich in Vitamin A that it's poisonous to humans?

8 WEDNESDAY

Today in AD632 the Prophet Mohammad died – but the Islamic faith he established goes on. When plans were made to introduce identity cards in Kenya the authorities ran into a problem. The modest Moslem women who normally wore veils refused to have their photos taken in case they had to show them to strange men.

And did you know that . . .
In 1975 the makers of the American version of Monopoly printed almost twice as much paper money as the US mint?
A number of geese on the ground are called a gaggle, but once in the air they are a skein?

9 THURSDAY

Cole Porter, sophisticated and cynical song-writer, was born today in 1891. In 1937 his legs were crushed in a riding accident. While he waited in agony for help, he passed the time by writing a song.

And did you know that . . .
There are around 3 million species of animal on Earth?
Caligula's horse Incitatus had his own retinue of slaves?

JUNE 1988

10
FRIDAY

59 years ago today the first Oxford and Cambridge boat race was held. Oxford won.

And in 1922 Judy Garland was born. She was signed to a movie contract with MGM at the age of 13, but the company was worried by her tendency to put on weight. Whenever she gained a few pounds she was put on a diet of chicken soup and amphetamines.

And did you know that . . .
White elephants are not white? They are grey with pink eyes.

11
SATURDAY

A year ago Margaret Thatcher became the first Prime Minister for 150 years to be elected for a third term. She's a great believer in getting value for money, but did you know that as a young scientist she worked on ways of mixing air into ice cream – so that the customers paid for more air and less ice-cream?

And did you know that . . .
The Russian name for Moscow is Finnish in origin?
The star is the most common shape to appear on flags?

12
SUNDAY

Three years ago today, in an attempt to shame manufacturers into improving standards, the Russians staged a display of shoddy goods. The star exhibit was a pair of boots with high heels attached to the *toes*!

And did you know that . . .
Frederick the Great liked his coffee made with champagne instead of water?
During the eighteenth century bear grease was used as a hair restorer?
St Jerome is the patron saint of opticians?

NOTES

On Margaret Thatcher...

I don't agree with all Margaret Thatcher's policies – basically I'd have to go along with other people for housing and the health service – but she's right about cutting the top rate of tax. Not many people know that the top rate of tax is now 60 per cent; a few years ago it used to be 82 per cent. They take £127 million more in top-rate tax now than they did when the tax was 82 per cent! (11 June)

JUNE 1988

13 MONDAY

Today in 323BC Alexander the Great died. His army numbered at the most 35,000 men, yet he never lost a battle and eventually ruled an empire that stretched all the way from Italy to India. One reason for his success was that before a battle he insisted that his soldiers' beards be shaved off so that their enemies couldn't grab hold of them.

And did you know that . . .
The Dead Sea is gradually rising?
The Japanese have no names for the months – they use numbers instead?

14 TUESDAY

Today three years ago a survey on pubs revealed that drinkers pay £320 a year for the froth on their beer. And frothy beer is more popular in the north of England than in the south.

And did you know that . . .
A woman in Miami drowned after drinking so much water she couldn't breathe?
The Burkut golden eagle is trained to hunt wolves and deer?
There are said to be as many as 10,000 different credit cards available in the USA?

15 WEDNESDAY

Today in 1890 the first film review was inspired by the first screen kiss. The movie was called *The Widow Jones* and the kissing couple were May Irwin and John Rice. The review described their close encounter as 'absolutely disgusting'.

And did you know that . . .
The term 'Siamese twins' was only introduced in 1811 after Chang and Eng, joined twins from Siam (now Thailand), became famous?
The desert lynx catches birds in mid-flight by jumping into the air?

16 THURSDAY

Today is Bloom's Day. The entire action of James Joyce's famous *Ulysses* – a day in the life of Leopold Bloom – took place on 16 June 1904. Joyce is estimated to have had a working vocabulary of around 30,000 words. That's the same as Shakespeare and about four times as many as most of us.

And did you know that . . .
The sperm whale stuns its prey by 'shouting' at it?

JUNE 1988

17 FRIDAY

Three years ago today jeweller Kenneth Markworth was about to set a £7,000 diamond in a ring when raiders dashed into his shop. Rather than hand over the gem Mr Markworth swallowed it. It's not on record whether he was able to get it back later.

And did you know that . . .
The first Spanish dog to be fitted with contact lenses was killed the following day as it tried to cross the road?
In 1929 a patent was issued for a device to create artificial dimples in the cheeks?

18 SATURDAY

Four years ago today Joyce McKinney was at it again. In 1977 she hit the British headlines after being accused of kidnapping a Mormon missionary and forcing him to have sex. Seven years later she still hadn't forgotten him and was again arrested for pestering him at his place of work.

And did you know that . . .
The first fish in space was a South American guppie?
Japanese women wear special padded underwear to make their flat bottoms look more rounded?

19 SUNDAY

The South Pole has moved – and that's official. Three years ago today it was announced that the South Pole had shifted towards Australia and is around 90 miles from the Antarctic coastline. Although the North Pole is a fixed point, the South Pole drifts continuously and is plotted every five years or so.

And did you know that . . .
Cold showers tend to increase sexual arousal?
Bees can see ultraviolet light?
In 1888 a hailstorm in Moradabad, India, killed an estimated 246 people?

NOTES

On Film Reviews...

The Swarm, a disaster movie which I made in 1979, had some really bad reviews but there's no such thing as a total flop. It made enough money to enable me to buy a house in America!

JUNE 1988

20 MONDAY

The world's longest sausage, all 9.8 miles of it, was cooked one year ago today in Hyde Park as part of the celebrations for the centenary of the St John Ambulance Brigade.

And did you know that . . .
Ducks only lay eggs in the early morning?
*   In mediaeval France ordinary people were allowed to wear shoes with points between six and twelve inches long, while princes had two-foot-long points?*
*   Diamonds burn if heated above 1,400 degrees Fahrenheit?*

21 TUESDAY

Jane Russell is 67 today. 'There are two good reasons why men will go to see her,' said Howard Hughes, who spotted her while she was working as a dental assistant and immediately recognized the potential of her magnificent bosom. And to make sure that her attributes weren't ignored he designed a special cantilevered bra for her first film, *The Outlaw*.

And did you know that . . .
The Greek national anthem has 158 verses?
*   The tuna fish has to keep swimming, otherwise it suffocates?*

22 WEDNESDAY

1988 is a Leap Year and so the Summer Solstice is celebrated today. In a normal year it would have been observed yesterday. The most famous celebrations go on at Stonehenge, where Druids and hippies vie to watch the midsummer sun rise over the stones. Not many people know that the monument had been standing for 1,000 years before the Druids were established.

And did you know that . . .
Two-thirds of the tea drunk in eighteenth-century England had been smuggled into the country to avoid tax?

23 THURSDAY

Two years ago today it was reported that the first official dromedary dairy had been set up in Saudi Arabia. There was plenty of demand for the milk which was being sold at £1.20 a litre.

And did you know that . . .
An ancient Egyptian form of contraception involved applying a mixture of honey, soda and crocodile dung?

JUNE 1988

Flying saucers were born 41 years ago today after Kenneth Arnold, who was looking for missing aircraft, spotted nine shiny discs zooming through the sky. When questioned about them by the press he described them as looking 'like a saucer', and flying saucers they've been ever since.

And did you know that . . .

To get the sound of someone's head being chopped off, the BBC sound effects department uses a sharp knife and large white cabbage?

25 SATURDAY

George Orwell was born today in 1903. His real name was Eric Blair and he was educated at Eton before becoming an honorary member of the working class.

And did you know that . . .

Tabby cats are named after a type of striped Turkish cloth known as attabi?

Moss Bros. once supplied a Danish department store with 50 bowler hats which were used to hold flowerpots in a window display?

There are more ants than any other kind of social insect in the world?

26 SUNDAY

Three years ago a court in Edinburgh heard the tale of the robot wine waiter who ran riot in a restaurant. Rather than serving drinks, as it had been programmed to do, it ran amok, knocking over furniture and terrifying diners until its head fell off into a customer's lap.

And did you know that . . .

Etienne de Silhouette, after whom the silhouette is named, was a highly unpopular eighteenth-century French finance minister?

NOTES

On Technology . . .

My father originally wanted me to follow him into fish-portering, but when Billingsgate went over to machines he changed his mind and warned me never to take a job they could invent a machine to do. I figured that no-one could invent a machine to take over from actors – not in my lifetime anyway!

(26 June)

JUNE 1988

27 MONDAY

Today in 1746 Bonnie Prince Charlie escaped to Skye with Flora MacDonald. For safety he went in the disguise of an Irish maid named Betty Burke, and wore a flowery frock and apron.

And did you know that . . .

In ancient Greece an hour was defined as one-twelfth of the day? Hours were longer in summer than winter.

Birds have almost no sense of smell?

The meter is not an arbitrary measure, like the yard? It is based on the length of 1,533,164.12 light waves.

28 TUESDAY

Three years ago today it was reported that Ruth Lawrence intended to study for her doctorate in maths at Oxford University. Nothing so special about that – except that she was 13 at the time and had already passed her bachelor degree with more than double the marks required to win her a coveted starred first.

And did you know that . . .

Until 1700 the world's coffee was grown only in Arabia and coffee plants were not allowed out of the country?

The Vatican library contains some volumes written on human skin?

29 WEDNESDAY

Two years ago today Richard Branson captured the Blue Riband for his record crossing of the Atlantic. He did it in 3 days, 8 hours and 31 minutes, despite a problem when someone filled the petrol tanks with water.

And did you know that . . .

There is less absenteeism in air-conditioned offices than in offices without air-conditioning?

Large areas of the Arabian Desert have not been properly mapped?

St Bernards have never carried red barrels of brandy around their necks? This idea was invented by Sir Edwin Landseer in one of his paintings.

30 THURSDAY

Today in 1936 *Gone with the Wind* by Margaret Mitchell was published and became a best-seller. When it was turned into a movie the properties department had to find a record-breaking 1,250,000 items to set the scenes.

JULY 1988

1 FRIDAY

Four years ago it was reported that Venetian pigeons had been put on the Pill. In an attempt to reduce their numbers, contraceptives were mixed with the grain normally scattered for them.

And did you know that . . .
The first British criminal to be convicted on the evidence of his fingerprints was put away in 1902?
From the peak of Mount Izaru in Costa Rica you can see both the Pacific and Atlantic oceans?

2 SATURDAY

Today in 1984 a Canadian became the first person to go over Niagara Falls in a barrel since 1961. He escaped with minor cuts and bruises. Amazingly, the first person ever to try this stunt was a woman – and she couldn't swim.

And did you know that . . .
The largest of all measures of champagne, the nebuchadnezzar, contains five gallons of bubbly?
Amstrad word processors are known to their owners as 'Joyce'?

3 SUNDAY

The Leaning Tower of Pisa's tilt increased by ·4mm in the year 1983-4, according to a report published four years ago today.

And did you know that . . .
During the hula-hoop craze in the 1950s, hula-hoops were banned in Japan because of the number of traffic accidents and back injuries they caused?
A Chinese priest let his fingernails grow for 27 years?
Soap was introduced to this country by the Romans, yet wasn't in common use until the seventeenth century?

NOTES

_____

_____

_____

THINGS TO DO IN JULY:

_____

JULY 1988

4 MONDAY

Today is Independence Day in the USA and it's also the day on which three American presidents died. They were John Adams, Thomas Jefferson and James Monroe.

And did you know that . . .

Baby rattlesnakes are just as poisonous as full-grown ones?
You share your birthday with at least 9 million other people?
Until 1984 Belgians had to choose their children's names from 1,500 officially approved ones drawn up during the Napoleonic era?

5 TUESDAY

Two years ago today the Malaysian Telecommunications minister dialled the newly-registered millionth subscriber to offer his congratulations. He got a wrong number.

And did you know that . . .

Chop Suey was invented in New York, not China?
In 1783 a duck, a sheep and a rooster flew in a hot air balloon in front of Louis XVI and Marie Antoinette?
An IBM personal computer has about the same degree of intelligence as a beetle?

6 WEDNESDAY

The Bayeux tapestry is English! Today in 1984 experts carefully unstitched the lining of this 900-year-old piece of embroidery and confirmed that only English embroiderers had the skill to work so neatly.

And did you know that . . .

Traditionally, circus clowns have unique make-up patterns? A clown established his face by painting the pattern on a eggshell and then registering it. On his death the shell is broken.

7 THURSDAY

Pierre Cardin, French fashion designer, is 66 today. He once tried on the space suit that Neil Armstrong wore when he walked on the moon. No one else has ever been allowed to wear it.

And did you know that . . .

The Israeli government set up a camel hospital in 1978?
It's been estimated that 65 per cent of the world's population doesn't read newspapers, listen to the radio or watch TV?
You can have your car blessed by a Buddhist monk in Tokyo?

JULY 1988

8
FRIDAY

John McEnroe won the Men's Singles final at Wimbledon today in 1984. It was the first time in the history of the tournament that all the defending champions had successfully retained their titles and all the number one seeds had won.

And did you know that . . .

Pontefract in Yorkshire used to be surrounded by fields growing licorice?
    You cannot be excommunicated from the Hindu religion?
    Pillar boxes were originally painted green?

9
SATURDAY

The first Chinese-language edition of *Playboy* was published in Hong Kong in 1986. All 50,000 copies had been sold by the end of the day.

And did you know that . . .

When Arabs shake their heads they mean yes?
    Bagpipes were played in Persia, Egypt and Greece long before the Scots adopted them from the Romans?
    In 85 per cent of men the left testicle hangs lower than the right?

10
SUNDAY

James McNeill Whistler was born today in 1934. He's most famous for the painting known as 'Whistler's Mother', but in fact the work is entitled *An Arrangement in Black and Grey* (The Artist's Mother). He was also famous for his arrogance. Once he ordered some blank canvases to be sent to him. They were lost in the mail and when he complained and was asked if they were of any great value he replied, 'Not yet.'

And did you know that . . .

It has been estimated that if the world's surplus grain were to be stored in a plastic pipe 1ft in diameter, it would stretch around the world 600 times?

NOTES

On *Playboy* . . .

I've read *Playboy* in my time, and years ago I stayed at the Playboy mansion at the invitation of Hugh Heffner. I asked him how he knew me, because I wasn't that well known in America then. He told me that *Zulu* was one of his all-time favourite films! (9 July)

JULY 1988

11 MONDAY

One of the few Mongolians to become a Hollywood star, Yul Brynner was born today in 1915. He made his name in *The King and I* playing King Mongut of Siam. Not many people know that Mongut had 9,000 wives and concubines.

And did you know that . . .
Russian birth records include details of a pair of twins patriotically called Anarchy and Utopia?
Fewer than 10 species of shark are capable of eating humans?

12 TUESDAY

74 years ago Professor Hans Friedenthal of Berlin University described the things that would happen to the emancipated woman. He predicted that she would become bald and grow a moustache and long beard. Strangely enough, experts have discovered that working women who suffer from stress *do* tend to develop excess facial hair and sometimes go thin on top.

And did you know that . . .
The harp is the only stringed instrument in an orchestra which isn't played with a bow?

13 WEDNESDAY

According to a report published four years ago today, oil-rich residents of Jeddah, Saudi Arabia, have the highest number of cars per family in the world. There were nearly five cars for every family.

And did you know that . . .
The only film to have been made in Latin was Dereck Jarman's homosexual epic Sebastiane?
Queen Elizabeth I bathed once a month – whether she needed to or not?

14 THURSDAY

Tragedy struck Karlsruhe Zoo in West Germany today in 1984. Two hippos died of panic after Rani the Indian elephant turned on a hot water valve with her trunk and sent a cascade of boiling water into their pool. By the time the staff arrived the heat in the hippo enclosure had reached 150 degrees Fahrenheit.

And did you know that . . .
The QWERTY typewriter keyboard is not the most efficient? It was designed to slow down typists because early machines couldn't cope.

JULY 1988

15 FRIDAY

Today is St Swithin's Day and myth has it that if it rains today it will rain for the next 40, too. It all goes back to 971AD when Swithin's remains were moved from a grave outside Winchester Cathedral to a shrine inside, after which it rained for 40 days. Fortunately records show that there's no truth in the saying . . .

And did you know that . . .

Richard I spent only six months of his 10-year reign in England?
   An American judge was dismissed from the bench after using a dildo instead of a gavel?

16 SATURDAY

Today is Ginger Rogers's 77th birthday. Not many people know that she started as a big-band singer before she teamed up with Fred Astaire. They were the perfect partners, as Katharine Hepburn noted: 'He gives her class, she gives him sex.'

And did you know that . . .

The fingers and toes are the coldest parts of the body?
   Around a thousand people commit suicide every day worldwide?
   Houston, Texas, is built on a swamp and is slowly sinking?

17 SUNDAY

33 years ago the first Disneyland opened in California. These days the only capital city to boast a Disneyland is Tokyo. Not many people know that although Disney himself had a moustache, no one who worked for him was allowed to grow one.

And did you know that . . .

The first sleeve buttons were sewn on to the front of soldiers' jacket sleeves to prevent them from wiping them across their faces? Gradually the buttons moved to the back of the sleeve and became merely decorative.

NOTES

On Walt Disney . . .

The first Disney cartoon I saw was *Bambi* and it made me cry. As a child I spent almost my entire life at the cinema, but not watching Disney films. It was the Lone Ranger, Tarzan, things like that – Walt Disney was a bit cissy for where I lived. (17 July)

JULY 1988

18 MONDAY

Two years ago it was announced from San Diego, California, that an attempt to build the world's largest sand castle had been cancelled – due to lack of sand.

And did you know that . . .

Chewing gum is banned in Singapore because of the cost of removing it from floors and furniture?

Coca-Cola makes an efficient contraceptive douche?

Spencer Perceval is the only British prime minister to have been assassinated in office?

19 TUESDAY

A report published today in 1986 from a number of US airlines revealed the kind of things that people try to take on planes as hand luggage. Among the items were a 10-foot artificial tree, a grandfather clock, a car door, an ironing board, a life-sized stuffed toy pony, a 500lb computer and a full-sized pinball machine.

And did you know that . . .

Juicy Fruit and Doublemint were the first brands of Wrigley's chewing gum?

Brazil was the second country in the world to produce postage stamps?

20 WEDNESDAY

The first 'modern' book on plastic surgery, written by a Venetian called Tagliacozzi in 1597, was sold four years ago to Sotheby's for £11,500. The author was the world's earliest pioneer of plastic surgery and after his death this particular branch of medicine was ignored for another 200 years.

And did you know that . . .

Iceland has no railway or army?

21 THURSDAY

In 1920 young Elsie Wright became famous after photographing fairies in her garden in Cottingley, Yorkshire. Experts declared the pictures genuine; Sir Arthur Conan Doyle took them as proof of the spirit world; scores of people confirmed that they'd seen fairies too. The pictures were a mystery for many years and Elsie always insisted that they were genuine. Then two years ago today she confessed all. The fairies were made of paper and had been stuck to the ground; the creator of the great Sherlock Holmes had been fooled by amateur trick photography!

JULY 1988

22 FRIDAY

Four years ago today Jim Fixx, the high priest of jogging, died – while out jogging.

And did you know that . . .

Many African tribes use ants to 'stitch' together wounds? The ants clamp the wound with their teeth; when their bodies are pulled off, their jaws stay in place.

23 SATURDAY

Raymond Chandler, author of *The Big Sleep*, was born a hundred years ago today. While he wrote detective stories his wife Cissy got on with the housework – in the nude.

And did you know that . . .

President Harry Truman was crazy about playing poker?
*   Baby whales can grow at the rate of 10lb per hour?*
*   Egyptians mummified their dead cats and buried them with mummified mice, so that in the afterworld they would have something to chase?*

24 SUNDAY

Bob Geldof, the Irish organizer of Band Aid, was knighted two years ago today. He didn't shave for the occasion but the Queen told him how smart he looked in his morning suit. Because he's not a British citizen the knighthood is an honorary one; he can't be called Sir Bob, but he is entitled to put the letters KBE after his name.

And did you know that . . .

King James IV of Scotland was the first monarch to play golf?
*   Fatty Arbuckle was the first person to receive a custard pie in the face on film?*

NOTES

On Plastic Surgery...

I haven't had plastic surgery or a face lift and I never will. Aging is natural, you have to accept it. I remember Tommy Cooper saying, 'My wife's just had her face lifted, but it's not lifted far enough – I can still see her'!
(20 July)

On Peerages...

Most of the honours people get awarded are okay but I think we should get rid of hereditary peerages; the number of berks who end up in the House of Lords – you know, that's why they call it *Burke's Peerage!*
(24 July)

JULY 1988

25 MONDAY

Four years ago today Mr Glyn 'Scotty' Wolfe, aged 76, filed for divorce – his 26th. Undeterred by his latest failure, Mr Wolfe was soon on the lookout for wife number 27.

And did you know that . . .
Bombay has more video libraries than any other city in the world – around 15,000 at the last count?
Cucumbers really are cool? On a warm day the centre of a cucumber is about 20 degrees Fahrenheit cooler than the air temperature.

26 TUESDAY

According to the finidings of a survey published two years ago today, the stereotyped image of a tax official – a middle-aged man in a grey suit – is all wrong. The typical tax official of 1986 was a woman between the ages of 21 and 25.

And did you know that . . .
The only feature film to have been made in Esperanto was Incubus, *made in 1965 and starring 'Star Trek' actor William Shatner?*
Mark Twain is said to have been the first author to send his publisher a typewritten manuscript?

27 WEDNESDAY

Hilaire Belloc, prolific author of all kinds of book, from novels and verse to travelogues, was born today in 1902. Much of his work was done in haste to make money and did not please him. On one train journey he found a fellow passenger reading *The History of England* which he had written. He asked the man how much he had paid for it, gave him the money and then threw the book out of the window.

And did you know that . . .
A human sneeze contains up to 85 million viruses emitted at more than 100 miles an hour over a distance of up to 12 feet?

28 THURSDAY

26 years ago today the Mariner I space probe was launched from Cape Canaveral, its destination Venus. After just four minutes in flight it crashed into the Atlantic. A post mortem showed that a minus sign had been left out of the instructions fed into the computer – a human error that cost more than £4 million.

JULY 1988

29 FRIDAY

Today in 1890 Vincent Van Gogh died after shooting himself two days previously. It was said that during the last seventy desperate days of his life he painted seventy pictures.

And did you know that . . .

As well as the light bulb and the gramophone, Edison also constructed the first electric typewriter?
The first airborne celebration of Mass was said aboard the airship Hindenberg*?*

30 SATURDAY

22 years ago today England won the World Cup. Geoff Hurst was the man of the match – he scored a hat trick, the first player ever to do so in a World Cup final.

And did you know that . . .

The S in Harry S. Truman's name doesn't stand for anything?
Popcorn was invented by the American Indians?
In 1979 the average American woman bought five pairs of shoes?

31 SUNDAY

A Belgian businessman announced a new invention today in 1984. Designed for jet-setting Moselms, it was a prayer carpet with a working compass incorporated into its weave to ensure that wherever he found himself, the owner could guarantee facing Mecca.

And did you know that . . .

One of the students enrolled on a course about the life and music of the Beatles was Miss Penny Lane?
American golfers have bigger balls than British golfers?

NOTES

On Sport . . .

I play tennis – it's my only sport and I love it. My father was a very good tennis player too. I'm not a football fan, though I appeared in a picture called *Escape to Victory* with Pele and Bobby Moore. They kicked me to smithereens! (30 July)

THINGS TO DO IN AUGUST:

AUGUST 1988

1
MONDAY

Two years ago today a myth was exploded when Swiss historian Fritz Mathy Weist announced that Switzerland's national hero William Tell could not have shot an apple from his son's head with a crossbow. Crossbows were unknown in Switzerland in the thirteenth century.

And did you know that . . .

In 1938 a pilot took off from New York intending to fly to Los Angeles, turned the wrong way and ended up a day later in Ireland?
The kiwi has its nostrils at the end of its beak?

2
TUESDAY

Debonair British actor David Niven was buried today in 1983. Although he later became known as the archetypal Englishman, in his first 27 films he played nothing but Mexicans.

And did you know that . . .

Only one in five babies is born on the day predicted by doctors?
Margarine was invented by a scientist named Mege-Mouries?
The shortest war on record occurred in 1896 between England and Zanzibar? It lasted 38 minutes

3
WEDNESDAY

18 years ago today Mrs Miriam Hargrave passed her driving test at the fortieth attempt and after eight years of lessons. Eight years after she tore up her L-plates it was reported that she still didn't like making right-hand turns.

And did you know that . . .

The most popular cheese in the USA is Cheddar?
The local beer brewed on St Helena is called Atlantic ale?
President Marcos of the Philippines paid $50,000 for a 'painting' that was actually just an enlarged photo painted over?

4
THURSDAY

A museum of childhood in Derbyshire which had reconstructed a Victorian chimney so that schoolchildren could climb it and find out for themselves what chimney sweeping was like, had to abandon the idea two years ago today. Apparently modern children are more plump than their Victorian counterparts and they kept getting stuck in the flue.

And did you know that . . .

Marco Polo brought back the recipe for ice cream from China?

AUGUST 1988

5
FRIDAY

Two years ago the National Book League revealed the holiday reading it was sending to Balmoral for the royal family. Among them were thrillers by P.D. James and John Le Carré, a biography of Montgomery, an anthology of fishing literature for the Queen Mother and for Prince Harry a book called *Harry's Mad*.

And did you know that . . .
'Happy Birthday', the world's most widely-sung song, is still in copyright? Fortunately the copyright owners don't insist on royalties from private individuals.

6
SATURDAY

484 years ago today Archbishop Matthew Parker was born. He liked to keep an eye on what everyone was doing and he also had a very long nose – which is how the phrase 'nosey Parker' came to be coined.

And did you know that . . .
Ripe cranberries bounce? The best way to tell if they're ready for eating is to throw them on a hard floor; if they bounce like a golf ball, go ahead.
   The world's largest hotel was knocked down to build the Empire State Building?

7
SUNDAY

Miss Phyllis Newcombe, aged 22, was at a dance today in 1938 when she spontaneously combusted in front of a crowd of people.

And did you know that . . .
Kidney and gall bladder stones can now be 'exploded' using miniature bombs?
   Sir Isaac Newton named the colours of the rainbow?
   The Anaconda and the Serpent are types of musical instrument?
   Ice hockey was invented by the English when Kingston Harbour, Ontario, froze over in 1860?

NOTES

On Spontaneous Combustion...

I've never known anyone who's spontaneously combusted, but I know a few people I wish would!   (4 August)

AUGUST 1988

8 MONDAY

14 years ago today Richard Nixon resigned as President of the USA after the facts of the Watergate case became widely known. He was the only President on record to have worn a special steel 'celebrity glove' to make it easier to shake hands with the thousands of people he encountered on his political campaign.

And did you know that . . .
The whale shark lays the world's largest eggs?
Camels are born without humps?

9 TUESDAY

Today in 1902 Edward VII was crowned – six weeks after the original date set for the ceremony because he'd required an emergency appendectomy. Souvenir sellers were not pleased; they'd already had the coronation mugs decorated with the wrong date. More grateful were hundreds of East Enders who ate the perishable food that had originally been intended for the coronation banquet.

And did you know that . . .
The second most frequently used vowel in the English language is A?

10 WEDNESDAY

Today in 1895 saw the first night of the first Promenade Concert. It was conducted by Henry Wood at the Queen's Hall and a standing ticket cost 1s.

And did you know that . . .
The Rubik's Cube has 43,252,003,274,489,856,000 potential arrangements?
Donald Duck is referred to in the Vatican newspaper as Donald Anas?
Corrugated paper was originally invented for making hatbands?

11 THURSDAY

A report published five years ago today revealed that the Spanish custom of taking a siesta is going out of fashion. Only two out of ten Spaniards enjoy a nap after their midday meal.

And did you know that . . .
Coffee is the second largest commodity traded in the world? The biggest is oil.
Fish can suffer from seasickness?
Harrods' water supply is ensured by its three private wells?

AUGUST 1988

12
FRIDAY

It's the Glorious Twelfth today – the day that all grouse dread. In 1986 the restaurant of the Savoy Hotel excelled itself and offered freshly-shot grouse for lunch. The poor birds had been bagged at dawn, flown down from the moors by the Red Devils, dropped by parachute into the Royal Hospital, Chelsea, and then raced by boat along the Thames to the waiting chef.

And did you know that . . .

The nineteenth-century suburbs of Moscow are built on foundations of rubble and rubbish shipped to Russia from London?

13
SATURDAY

Five years ago today the staff of a Japanese zoo mourned the passing of their tiger, which was said to be the oldest in the world. It was 21. The average tiger lives to the age of 12.

And did you know that . . .

One nineteenth-Century Cardinal who worked as a librarian at the Vatican could speak 114 languages and many more dialects?
   Pearls are produced by shellfish other than oysters? The conch produces a particularly sought-after pink pearl.

14
SUNDAY

Today in Sweden it's Crayfish Day. By tonight the Swedes will have eaten around 3,000 tons of crayfish, all of them at least 20cm long and most of them imported from Turkey. Quite why crayfish have a special day to themselves, no one knows . . .

And did you know that . . .

The Chinese were the first people to use toilet paper?
   The most common name in the world is Mohammed?
   Masai tribesmen spit at each other when they meet? It's considered polite.

NOTES

On Grouse . . .

I eat grouse all the time and I love it. I'm the first one at the Connaught for the start of the season, but I couldn't shoot an animal. I'm not into all that hunting and shooting . . . I'm a complete hypocrite when it comes to that.   (12 August)

AUGUST 1988

15
MONDAY

Three years ago today 10-year-old Keith Byrne and his friend decided to have an adventure. They stowed away on the Dublin to Holyhead ferry, hitched their way from there to London, beat the security system at Heathrow and boarded an Air India jumbo jet where they watched a movie and ate dinner on their way to New York. The policeman who finally nabbed them as they tried to bluff their way through customs in the USA admired their nerve. 'They could both end up at the head of some large corporation,' he said.

16
TUESDAY

A West German bought a roll for his breakfast this morning in 1983, broke it open – and discovered a human finger. The bakery confirmed that a member of the staff had lost a digit; they'd searched the dough but, finding nothing, had decided to go ahead and bake it anyway.

And did you know that . . .
Shoe sizes were set down by Edward II in 1324? A size 13 shoe is equal in length to 39 barleycorns set in a row. There is one barleycorn difference between each standard shoe size.

17
WEDNESDAY

96 years ago today the outrageous Mae West was born. Her third movie was entitled *It Ain't No Sin* and to advertise it a publicist trained 50 parrots to repeat the title on cue. Then Catholic priests, objecting to Miss West's sexual innuendos, began to parade past the movie's posters with placards saying IT IS. To the dismay of the man who had done so much work with the parrots, the title of the film was changed to *The Belle of the Nineties*.

And did you know that . . .
The first American badminton club limited play on its courts to men and 'good-looking single women'?

18
THURSDAY

144 years ago Menelek II of Ethiopia was born. Whenever he felt ill he would eat a few pages of the Bible to make himself better. And he once ordered three electric chairs from America; only after they arrived did someone realize that Ethiopia at that time had no electricity . . .

And did you know that . . .
Franklin D. Roosevelt was once sent a telegram a quarter of a mile long?

AUGUST 1988

19 FRIDAY

An attempt two years ago today to roll down the Thames in a giant plastic bubble backfired when the bubble sprang a leak. The two men inside, who'd been rolling it along, had to be rescued.

And did you know that . . .
Amber is the fossilized resin of a prehistoric tree? It often contains tiny dead insects and animals.
The world's largest store of uncut diamonds is kept in Holborn, London?

20 SATURDAY

48 years ago today Winston Churchill made his famous speech praising the bravery of the RAF in the Battle of Britain. 'Never in the field of human conflict has so much been owed by so many to so few,' he said. In five days the outnumbered RAF destroyed 236 German planes for a loss of only 95.

And did you know that . . .
Charles II was the first English king to take an interest in small dogs which, until then, had been considered suitable for ladies?

21 SUNDAY

Today in 1614 Elizabeth Bathory died. Convinced that she could rejuvenate her aging body by bathing in the blood of young girls, she scoured the countryside around her castle in Hungary for victims, 610 were kidnapped and killed to supply the bloodbath. Eventually in 1610 someone discovered her secret and as punishment the countess was walled up in her room, where she died four years later.

And did you know that . . .
Every continent in the world contains a city called Rome?

NOTES

On the Second World War...

I loved the war – I must be about the only person who did! I grew up in Bermondsey and got evacuated to a farm in Norfolk. It gave me a first taste of freedom and country life, and I suppose my life now is aiming to recreate that. It's like a second childhood! I've got 10 acres and I'm very into ecology and organic gardening and that kind of thing – the countryside and the need for space for kids to play in are things I take seriously.

(20 August)

AUGUST 1988

22 MONDAY

Dorothy Parker was born today in 1893. Her wit and quick thinking were legendary. When asked to think of a sentence incorporating the word horticulture she instantly came back with, 'You can lead a horticulture but you can't make her think.'

And did you know that . . .
Some pumice stone floats on water?
*   International athletics races are always run in an anti-clockwise direction?*

23 TUESDAY

62 years ago today the Great Lover, Rudoph Valentino, died. For a man who had millions of women swooning, his love life was confused. Both his wives were lesbians and he once gave Ramon Novarro a black lead dildo.

And did you know that . . .
Northern Ireland suffers worse air pollution than any other part of the UK?
*   It takes 35 gallons of oil to make one barrel?*

24 WEDNESDAY

Today in 1875 Captain Matthew Webb became the first man to swim the English Channel. Since his achievement hundreds of others have attempted the crossing. They include people who've walked across on floats, windsurfed, water-skied, rowed across in a coffin and paddled across in an inner tube.

And did you know that . . .
In Salt Lake City, Utah, the automatic street crossings make bird call sounds to tell people when to cross?

25 THURSDAY

Leonard Bernstein, composer of *West Side Story*, is 70 today. His father was once accused of not offering him enough encouragement when he was growing up. 'How was I to know he would grow up to be Leonard Bernstein?' asked Bernstein senior.

And did you know that . . .
London's Science Museum is built over a maze designed by Prince Albert?
*   There are no turkeys in Turkey?*

AUGUST 1988

26 FRIDAY

The Mini, *the* car of the sixties, is 29 today. Also today, but in 55BC, Caesar first arrived in Britain.

And did you know that . . .
The first car ignition keys were introduced in 1949?
The giant Sony corporation's name is a cross between the word sonus, *meaning sound, and the phrase 'Sonny boy'?*
Emily Dickinson wrote more than a thousand poems, yet only seven were published in her lifetime?

27 SATURDAY

Samuel Goldwyn, Hollywood movie mogul, was born 106 years ago today. He was almost as famous for his sayings, called Goldwynisms, as for his movies. Among them were, 'A verbal contract isn't worth the paper it's written on', 'In two words, im–possible!' and 'I am willing to admit that I may not always be right, but I am never wrong.'

And did you know that . . .
Lord Nelson suffered from seasickness all his life?

28 SUNDAY

Five years ago today a couple in the Azairbaidjan area of Russia celebrated their 100th wedding anniversary. The wife was said to be 116, her husband 126.

And did you know that . . .
It would take one person about 30,000 years to count aloud to one trillion?
Bing Crosby used to stick his big ears to the side of his head with glue?

NOTES

On Marriage ...

I've got a basic morality that goes all the way back to the East End where I grew up. You can call it Victorian values if you like. I think love and respect are very important and I teach my daughters not to go out with men who don't respect them. As for these pre-nuptial agreements, they presuppose that the marriage won't work – so why bother with it? I think you have to have a complete commitment. A marriage is a contract in its own way.

AUGUST 1988

29 MONDAY

106 years ago today England's cricketers lost a Test Match for the first time, against Australia. In *The Times* the next day an obituary was published: 'In affectionate remembrance of English cricket, which died at the Oval... The body will be cremated and the ashes taken to Australia.' Thus the Ashes were born.

And did you know that . . .

The organ is a much older instrument than the piano?
The River Amazon has more than a thousand tributaries?
Electric fans warm up rather than cool the air?

30 TUESDAY

Mary Shelley, wife of poet Percy Bysshe, was born today in 1797. One summer while she, Shelley and Byron were staying in Switzerland they decided that they would all try their hands at writing a ghost story. Shelley didn't produce anything; Byron wrote a story about a vampire and threw it away before it was finished; and to everyone's surprise, Mary wrote the horror classic *Frankenstein*.

And did you know that . . .

Shirt buttonholes are vertical but pyjama jacket buttonholes are usually horizontal?

31 WEDNESDAY

20 years ago today Sir Garry Sobers became the first cricketer to hit six sixes with six balls. The unfortunate bowler was Malcolm Nash and the ball is now on display at Nottingham Museum.

And did you know that . . .

H.J. Heinz, inventor of the baked bean, actually invented 60 products but decided to advertise his goods with the phrase '57 Varieties' because he thought it sounded better?
Ebony was originally chosen for piano keys because it showed off the pale hands of lady players to best advantage?

NOTES

_____

_____

_____

THINGS TO DO IN SEPTEMBER:

_____

SEPTEMBER 1988

Edgar Rice Burroughs, creator of Tarzan, was born today in 1875. During the shooting of the first Tarzan movies, *Tarzan of the Apes*, a lion which was supposed to have been doped sprang at Elmo Lincoln who was playing the lead role. He stabbed at it and it died while the cameras kept rolling.

And did you know that . . .

Mrs E. Hodges of Alabama, USA, is the only person known to have been hit by a meteorite?

SEPTEMBER 1988

2 FRIDAY

322 years ago today the Great Fire of London started in Pudding Lane in the city. The Lord Mayor was called out to take a look at the flames and in one of the great misjudgements of history declared, 'Pish! A woman might piss it out.' Four days later 80,000 people were homeless and 87 parish churches had been destroyed. Miraculously only eight people were killed.

And did you know that . . .
The Black Death, or bubonic plague to give it its proper name, is still killing people?
*   Underwater hockey is known as octopush?*

3 SATURDAY

Oliver Cromwell died 330 years ago today. His body was due to be embalmed for a state funeral but the process didn't work and the smell was so bad he had to be buried quickly. When, three years later, Charles II returned to the throne, he had the body dug up, publicly hung from a gallows, then decapitated. The head was put on a spike outside Westminster Hall and stayed there until 1680 when it blew off and a sentry took it home.

And did you know that . . .
The male star of Deep Throat *insured himself against getting any of his co-stars pregnant?*

4 SUNDAY

Three years ago today the most famous traffic warden in the world retired. Meta Davis put a parking ticket on Paul McCartney's car in 1967; he stopped her and asked her name and the result was the song 'Lovely Rita' about a meter maid.

And did you know that . . .
St Brigid of Ireland is said to have turned her used bathwater into beer?
*   Golfballs were originally made of leather stuffed with feathers?*

NOTES

On London . . .

I was born in London, I know it extremely well, and I love it. I think it's great that the East End and the docks are being developed; it's bringing in new jobs. Everyone complains that good old Cockney people are being pushed out of their own homes but in actual fact they're building on derelict areas where no one lived.

SEPTEMBER 1988

5 MONDAY

Four years ago today the Paris-Venice Orient Express train ground to a halt and was delayed for 40 minutes in Innsbruck after a woman got her foot stuck in the emergency brake handle – while making love.

And did you know that . . .
The giraffe was first known to English-speaking discoverers as the camelopard?
    The man who wrote 'I Left My Heart in San Francisco' died there?

6 TUESDAY

Salvador Dali, who had been badly burned after a fire in his twelfth-century castle near Gerona, was taken to hospital for treatment today. His life as well as his paintings have a touch of the surreal. His wife once asked him to paint a screen that could be used to hide an ugly radiator at the castle. Dali duly painted the screen – with a picture of the radiator.

And did you know that . . .
An ant can lift 50 times its own body weight?

7 WEDNESDAY

The Free Library of Trenton, USA had cause to celebrate three years ago today. A library book that had been missing for 188 years was finally returned. No one tried to add up the cost of the fine.

And did you know that . . .
The ice cream sundae was invented specially to be eaten on Sundays when ice cream sodas were banned?
    Boy Eskimos are taught to smoke a pipe at the earliest possible age – often three years?

8 THURSDAY

Today in 1199 Richard I, better known as Lionheart, died. He has always had a romantic reputation but it wasn't borne out in fact; he was homosexual, and when food supplies ran low on the crusades he had prisoners slaughtered and ate them.

And did you know that . . .
The duckbilled platypus is technically a mammal, yet it lays eggs, has webbed reptilian feet and carries a poisonous sting?
    The badger is the largest carnivorous mammal in the British Isles?

SEPTEMBER 1988

9 FRIDAY

87 years ago today Henri de Toulouse-Lautrec died. As a child he broke both thighs in separate accidents and his legs failed to develop properly. He also suffered from a condition called hypertrophy which gave him coarse-looking features and a penis so large in proportion to the rest of him that Parisian prostitutes called him 'Teapot'.

And did you know that . . .

The famous Manikin Pis statue in Brussels has been presented with a number of outfits and uniforms – one from Napoleon?

Red rain, caused by red Sahara dust, falls frequently throughout Europe?

10 SATURDAY

Arnold Palmer is 50 today. He started playing golf at the age of five and became the world's first golf millionaire. But it wasn't all success. One Los Angeles golf course has a plaque commemorating Palmer's achievement in the 1961 Los Angeles Open. It's situated on the par-five ninth hole and no, it doesn't celebrate a hole in one – it celebrates the 12 dismal strokes he took!

And did you know that . . .

More than 500 songs and musical pieces have been written about or dedicated to Abraham Lincoln?

11 SUNDAY

73 years ago today the first Welsh branch of the Women's Institute was founded in Llanfairpwllgwyngyllgogerychwyrndrobwllantysil-iogogogoch.

And did you know that . . .

The Hershey Bar, made in Hershey, USA, is the world's best-selling chocolate bar?

Billy the Kid killed 21 people before he was 21 years old?

The aubergine is technically a fruit – it's a member of the tomato family?

NOTES

_____

_____

_____

_____

SEPTEMBER 1988

12 MONDAY

A survey published in a women's magazine five years ago revealed that the average Scottish couple make love one more time each week than the average English couple. It also revealed that the living room is the most popular place for sex, that 1 in 100 couples do it on the stairs and that only 1 in 20 ever do it outdoors.

And did you know that . . .
Chinese women initially had their feet bound to keep them faithful? The binding process effectively crippled them and prevented them from running away with another man?

13 TUESDAY

Claudette Colbert, star of *It Happened One Night*, was born today in 1903. She believed that the left-hand side of her face photographed better than her right and always insisted on being filmed from that side – which was tough on her co-stars if they had the same problem.

And did you know that . . .
The longest descent by escalator is made in the Leningrad underground railway system where commuters descend 195ft?
    An electric eel can produce 550 volts?

14 WEDNESDAY

There was good news for Spanish schoolchildren four years ago today when homework was banned in primary and secondary schools.

And did you know that . . .
Of all the species of mammals that have become extinct in the last 1,900 years, around 70 per cent have died out in the last hundred years?
    The Swedes read more newspapers than the people of any other nation?
    The only two English words than contain the vowels in their correct order are abstemious *and* facetious?

15 THURSDAY

10 years ago today at the Superdome, New Orleans, Muhammad Ali proved he was the greatest yet again and won back his world title from Leon Spinks. Spinks had the distinction of holding the title for the shortest time in heavyweight boxing history – just 214 days.

And did you know that . . .
Until 1836 vanilla could only be grown in Mexico?

SEPTEMBER 1988

16
FRIDAY

Today three years ago in Paris the ancient Pont Neuf bridge was wrapped in 430,000 square feet of stone-coloured cloth in a project costing £1.5 million. It wasn't done to preserve the stone but as a work of art, designed by Christo Javacheff. Two weeks later it was unwrapped again.

And did you know that . . .
Mules are sterile?
*   The first toilet on board a plane was provided in 1931?*
*   The average person produces around 100 gallons of sewage each year?*

17
SATURDAY

Today in 1985 jelly-babies were withdrawn from sale in West Germany after traces of illegal sweetener, based on anti-freeze, were discovered in them.

And did you know that . . .
The Venus flytrap feeds mainly on ants, not flies?
*   The first licence number plates for cars were introduced in France in 1893?*
*   Dallas/Fort Worth airport covers a larger area than the whole of Manhattan?*
*   Rolex watches are hand-made and timed against an atomic clock?*

18
SUNDAY

Five years ago a Morse code message, relayed by powerful flashing lights, was sent 150 miles from mountain-top to mountain-top. It was a record distance for a visual message.

And did you know that . . .
The Empress Josephine, wife of Napoleon, was so fond of roses that at Malmaison she grew every known variety?
*   Human beings shed and replace their outer layer of skin every 28 days?*

NOTES

On Fussy Film Stars . . .

Rex Harrison was another actor who could only be filmed from one side. You start out thinking, 'What a conceited bloke . .' but you find they're right – they look awful if you photograph them from the other angle. Me, I don't have a best side. Well I do – but I'm sitting on it!

(13 September)

SEPTEMBER 1988

19 MONDAY

A survey of America's richest citizens was published four years ago today. It revealed that the richest individual was Gordon Peter Getty who had a fortune of $3.3 billion. Michael Jackson didn't make the top 400 because at the time he was worth only $70 million. Bob Hope, who *had* been included in the top 400, was dropped because he was only worth $115 million.

And did you know that . . .
Women are barred from Mount Athos in Greece? Some of the monastic communities there also ban female animals and birds.

20 TUESDAY

Today in 1985 Mr Hilton Mortin's toilet blew up. He'd made the mistake of cleaning it with two different chemicals; they reacted together and – BOOM!

And did you know that . . .
The legs of Japanese billiard tables are shorter than those of billiard tables used in the West?
Cary Grant was originally tipped to play James Bond?
The Foreign Legion march at 88 steps a minute?

21 WEDNESDAY

11 years ago today Victor the giraffe died after attempts to get him back on his feet failed. He'd done the splits while apparently trying to make love to a female giraffe, and couldn't get up. A winch was brought in and Victor was strapped into a canvas harness, but the tension was too much for him and his heart failed.

And did you know that . . .
The largest bird in the world, the ostrich, weighs 48,000 times as much as the smallest – the bee hummingbird?

22 THURSDAY

Way back in 1478 Philip the Handsome of Spain was born today. His wife was so distraught when he died that she kept his corpse and slept with it in her bed for three years. Not surprisingly she became known as Joanna the Mad.

And did you know that . . .
There was a canal connecting the Mediterranean to the Red Sea long before the Suez Canal was built? It was dug by the Persian King Darius around 525BC and was in use for several centuries.

SEPTEMBER 1988

23
FRIDAY

Mickey Rooney was born today in 1922. At the last count he'd been married eight times to, among others, Ava Gardner and Lana Turner. 'I'm the only man in the world who has a marriage licence made out To Whom It May Concern,' he once said.

And did you know that . . .

A poll taken in Morocco in 1969 revealed that 12 per cent of the population didn't know that man had landed on the Moon?
In 1978 the average American sent 20 Christmas cards?

24
SATURDAY

53 years ago today the first Jaguar car went on sale. It cost just £385. Also today, this time in 1984, Forestry Commission officials served venison and squirrel pie to people attending a conference on wildlife conservation at their centre in West Glamorgan.

And did you know that . . .

Translated literally, pot pourri *means 'putrid pot'?*
Rhododendron leaves are poisonous?
People who collect teddy bears are technically known as 'arctophiles'?

25
SUNDAY

One hundred years ago today a letter from a man who had murdered prostitute Mary Anne Nichols was delivered to the Central News Agency. It was signed 'Yours truly Jack the Ripper'. Having christened himself, Jack the Ripper became one of the most notorious criminals in British history – but without the name he would probably have been soon forgotten.

And did you know that . . .

It took 5,000 calf-skins to bind the 30 copies of the Gutenberg Bible printed in 1456?

NOTES

On Mickey Rooney...

I made a picture with Mickey Rooney – it was called *Pulp*. It wasn't a success for either of us but it was the turnabout of his career. He was really in the doldrums when we started but he never stopped working after that. He's a lovely man to work with – he's got lots of great jokes!　　　(23 September)

SEPTEMBER 1988

26
MONDAY

158 years ago in Massachusetts Colonel Robert Gibbon Johnson set out to prove to the superstitious locals that tomatoes weren't poisonous. His own doctor had warned him that after eating a couple he would froth at the mouth and develop appendicitis but, nothing daunted, the Colonel ate a whole basketful – with no ill-effects.

And did you know that . . .
Some parts of the Moon have been more carefully mapped than some parts of the Earth?

27
TUESDAY

Five years ago today the Americas Cup was handed over to Alan Bond, leader of the winning Australian syndicate that had broken America's 132-year monopoly of the world's most famous yacht race. As well as the cup Bond received a 3-foot bolt that had been used to screw the trophy to its stand – *permanently*, as the Americans had thought.

And did you know that . . .
In America it's fashionable to serve colourful vegetables, including red Brussels sprouts and mauve-and-white striped aubergines?

28
WEDNESDAY

Brigitte Bardot, sex-kitten turned animal-lover, is 54 today. 14 years ago she boasted in an interview that she 'must have a man every night'; now she lives alone and has dedicated herself to saving animals. A year ago she auctioned off her possessions to raise money with the words, 'I gave my beauty and youth to men. Now I am giving my wisdom and experience – the best part of me – to animals.'

And did you know that . . .
Spain, or Spania as it was originally called, means 'land of rabbits'?

29
THURSDAY

159 years ago the first Metropolitan policemen appeared on London streets. They wore top hats both to protect themselves and to stand on if they needed to look over high walls, and they carried football rattles which they sounded to summon help.

And did you know that . . .

The first four notes of Beethoven's Fifth Symphony spell the letter V in Morse code?

SEPTEMBER 1988

30 FRIDAY

James Dean died 33 years ago today when his Porsche Spyder crashed. Ironically just a few weeks before his death he'd made a public service film, advising youngsters to drive safely.

And did you know that . . .

The pigtail was banned in China in 1911 because it was a symbol of feudalism?

Lea and Perrins Worcestershire sauce is aged for two years before it is bottled?

NOTES

On the Police . . .

I don't think *all* **policemen should carry guns, but I think armed policemen should be available to respond quickly whenever they're needed . . .**

(29 September)

THINGS TO DO IN OCTOBER:

_____

_____

_____

_____

OCTOBER 1988

1 SATURDAY

The ever-wholesome Julie Andrews is 53 today. She dislikes her 'nice girl' image so much that she once wore a badge saying 'Mary Poppins is a Junkie'.

And did you know that . . .

Today in 1977 it was announced that you use 300 calories while making love and 12 calories in a passionate kiss?

Vexillology is the term for the study of flags?

When the X-ray was first invented a London department store developed a new line of X-ray-proof underwear for ladies nervous of being seen through?

2 SUNDAY

Today in 1890 zany comic genius Groucho Marx was born. He did a stint on a TV show called 'You Bet Your Life', where his sense of humour proved too raunchy for the small screen. On one occasion he interviewed a woman who had had twenty-two children: 'I love my husband,' she explained. 'I like my cigar too, but I take it out once in a while,' commented Groucho.

And did you know that . . .

The first man to fly in a glider was the coachman of Sir George Cayley, who offered his resignation when he returned safely to earth in 1853?

NOTES

On Julie Andrews...

The one thing I remember about Julie Andrews is that she *is* a bit like Mary Poppins. I remember going out to dinner once with her and she said, 'It's a cold night, where's your overcoat?' and I immediately went running back in and got it!   (1 October)

_____

_____

_____

_____

_____

_____

OCTOBER 1988

3 MONDAY

Six years ago it was reported in the press that baseball star Joe Dimaggio, once married to Marilyn Monroe, had cancelled his 20-year-old order for fresh flowers to be placed regularly on her tomb.

And did you know that . . .

Darts were originally developed as a form of self-defence for mediaeval archers, who threw them at the enemy when they got too close to use their arrows?

The human brain is about 80 per cent water?

4 TUESDAY

That great silent comedy clown Buster Keaton was born today in 1895. If you woke up with a hangover this morning why not try Keaton's favourite hangover cure? Take a glass of beer, break a raw egg into it, add a dollop of tomato ketchup, stir – and swallow.

And did you know that . . .

A 12-year-old Italian boy won a wrestling gold medal at the 1970 Edinburgh Commonwealth Games?

James Watt was twice arrested for 'flashing'?

5 WEDNESDAY

19 years ago today the history of British humour was revolutionized by the first episode of 'Monty Python's Flying Circus'.

And did you know that . . .

Film star Gloria Swanson once spent $9,000 on stockings and $6,000 on perfume in a single year?

On average we blink 25 times a minute?

Trees mentioned most often in the Bible are fig and cedar?

The lowest denomination banknote issued by the Bank of England was for one penny?

6 THURSDAY

The Jazz Singer, billed as the first feature-length 'talkie', was premiered in New York 61 years ago today. Al Jolson's words, 'You ain't heard nothin' yet' certainly electrified the audience, but there was in fact very little dialogue in the film. The first all-talking feature film was actually *The Lights of New York*.

And did you know that . . .

Winston Churchill and Clement Attlee had the same nanny?

In September 1983 an 11-year-old boy was elected Mayor of a Texas town?

OCTOBER 1988

7
FRIDAY

29 years ago today man first saw the dark side of the moon in pictures taken by Lunik III.

And in 1956 Clarence Birdseye died. He'd invented the process of deep-freezing food and revolutionized our eating habits.

And did you know that . . .

Al Capone had a bullet-proof office chair?
 Earmuffs were invented by Chester Greenwood in 1877?
 A drosometer is used to measure dew?

8
SATURDAY

In 1985 74 per cent of Europeans believed in God – that was the encouraging news relayed to Roman Catholic bishops today after they had commissioned a poll to find out whether this is a godless society or not.

And did you know that . . .

According to scientists, cold-blooded animals do not dream?
 A woman in the Huhan province of China can read with her buttocks?
 In America you can buy meat-flavoured toothpaste for dogs?

9
SUNDAY

They do everything very democratically in Liechtenstein. Three years ago it was decided to hold a referendum to decide a problem that had beset the principality for ages – where to site the public toilet.

And did you know that . . .

Humphrey Bogart wore size 10 shoes.?
 The phrase 'Hip, hip, hooray' was first used as a battle cry by knights at the Crusades?
 Fifty new toilets were installed at Buckingham Palace before Queen Victoria moved in, but very few of them actually worked?

NOTES

OCTOBER 1988

10 MONDAY

Orson Welles, who started his career so brilliantly with *Citizen Kane*, died three years ago today. He was very unhappy about his nose, which he felt to be too small for his face, and whenever he acted on stage he always wore a false one. During one performance of *Moby Dick* it began to come loose and eventually dropped off – at which Welles gave it a kick and launched it into the stalls.

And did you know that . . .
Your right lung takes in more air than your left lung?

11 TUESDAY

437 years after she set off from Portsmouth, the *Mary Rose* was returned there today in 1982. 700 people were believed to have been drowned when she sank in 1545.

And did you know that . . .
As a child, high-flyer Charles Lindbergh was afraid of heights?
*   Cheetahs were raced at Romford greyhound stadium in 1937?*
*   Dallas, Texas, is the most air-conditioned city in the world?*

12 WEDNESDAY

496 years ago today America was discovered by Christopher Columbus – according to legend, anyway. Although he landed in the West Indies, South America and Central America, he didn't set foot on what is known today as the USA. And as far as Columbus himself was concerned, he thought he was in Asia!

And did you know that . . .
Of the 'Swiss' cheese eaten in the US, more is imported from Austria and Finland than from Switzerland?
*   Around 10 per cent of the world's surface is covered with ice?*

13 THURSDAY

Happy Birthday to Prime Minister Margaret Thatcher, who is 63 today. Surprisingly for a woman renowned for her determination, she didn't think she'd make it to the top. In October 1969 after being appointed Shadow Spokesman on Education she said, 'No woman in my time will be PM or Chancellor or Foreign Secretary – not the top jobs. Anyway, I wouldn't want to be Prime Minister: you have to give yourself 100 per cent.'

And did you know that . . .
Redwood trees, which can grow higher than 300 feet, are the tallest living things on earth?

OCTOBER 1988

14
FRIDAY

Six years ago today an article in *The Times* revealed that Napoleon could have been killed by his wallpaper. When he died he was found to have a high level of arsenic in his blood and this led some people to believe he'd been poisoned. Research showed that the wallpaper in his room contained arsenic in the printing ink; if it got damp a fungus developed on the paper, releasing the arsenic into the air.

And did you know that . . .

The uniforms worn by Swiss guards at the Vatican are the oldest in the world? They were originally designed by Michelangelo.

15
SATURDAY

Mrs Betty Tudor tore up her L-plates today in 1982 after passing her driving test on the thirteenth attempt, 29 years after she first got behind the wheel and after being banned by three driving schools.

And did you know that . . .

Bulls chase clothed people but tend to ignore naked intruders?
    The first international language was not Esperanto but Volapuk, which was invented by an Austrian priest?
    Since the heyday of the British cinema four out of five Odeon sites have been closed?

16
SUNDAY

From the Soviet Central Statistical Board six years ago today came this description of the typical Russian man. He was called Alexander Kuznetsov (the most common name), was 5ft 7in tall, weighed 11st 2lb, lived in the city, worked in industry, read 21 books a year and went to evening classes. On average he spent less than 90 minutes a day watching TV. Russian women agreed with some of the findings but most said their husbands never read books or went to evening classes and they spent several hours a day slumped in front of the TV set.

And did you know that . . .

Sweden was the first country to use paper banknotes, which were introduced in 1661?

NOTES

On Orson Welles...

I'd love to play the Orson Welles part in *The Third Man*. It's my idea of a great role. You get all the kudos and you don't have to be there very long. That's the kind of role I'm looking for now!

OCTOBER 1988

17
MONDAY

Glamorous Rita Hayworth would have been 70 years old today. She was once discovered by Jack Lemmon tearing up a pile of unopened correspondence. 'Stop!' he told her. 'There may be cheques in there!'

Miss Hayworth just shrugged. 'There may,' she agreed. 'But there are also bills. I find it evens up.'

And did you know that . . .
In a lifetime the average human being breathes in 36,800 cubic metres of air, equivalent to 2.5 times the capacity of a large airship?

18
TUESDAY

Six years ago today the first recorded cattle grid complete with escape ramps for hedgehogs unlucky enough to fall in was installed on the A117 near Ludlow, Shropshire.

And did you know that . . .
It's said that only two men know the secret ingedient of Coca-Cola and that they never fly in the same plane?
Tennis was originally known as sphairistike?

19
WEDNESDAY

Marlon Brando made his stage debut 44 years ago today in *I Remember Broadway*. He was ruthless when it came to his performances. While filming *Mutiny on the Bounty* he made friends with an English bit-part actor and for the duration of the movie was almost inseparable from him. On the last day of filming the English actor wanted to swap addresses and keep in touch, but Brando told him to get lost. Offended, the Englishman wondered what he'd done. Then someone pointed out that in the movie Brando had played an Englishman – and that his English accent was based on that of his rejected 'friend'.

20
THURSDAY

20 years ago today Jacqueline Kennedy married Aristotle Onassis, but not before a 173-clause agreement had been drawn up and signed. According to this document the happy couple were to have no children and separate bedrooms. Jackie was to get £6,000 a month to spend on clothes and the promise of £6 million for each year of the marriage if Ari decided to leave her.

And did you know that . . .
Researchers doing a survey of the Copenhagen sex industry found a woman of 66 stripping to supplement her pension?

OCTOBER 1988

21
FRIDAY

Lord Nelson died 183 years ago today at the precise moment that the French and Spanish surrendered. His body was shipped home in a keg of brandy and the alcohol was tapped and topped up regularly in an effort to keep the remains fresh. It was believed by some that the sailors drank the discarded spirits.

And did you know that . . .

It has been estimated that the population of North America is carrying around more than 200,000,000 tons of excess fat?

22
SATURDAY

191 years ago today André-Jacques Garnerin became the first man to make a parachute jump. He flew to 2,000 feet in a balloon, then cut his basket free and floated to earth under an umbrella-shaped parachute. He survived and went on to give further parachuting displays.

And did you know that . . .

A menu of culinary favourites compiled in China in 1500BC reveals that swallows' tails and orang-utan's lips were popular?
In 1979 the banana was the best-selling fresh fruit in America?

23
SUNDAY

Three years ago newspapers reported that a factory in New Orleans had burned down. The factory made fire extinguishers.

And did you know that . . .

In Montana, USA, a 13-year-old boy was employed by his school to teach his teachers about computers?
The VW Beetle was one of Hitler's pet projects and was the first European car to sell more than a million?
Tooth decay is the most common disease in the world?

NOTES

On Making Money...

I'm involved in all sorts of business but the best investment of all has been the London restaurant, Langan's, which I set up 11 years ago. Funnily enough it's what they call a fun investment, but penny for penny it's made me more money than any other.

(17 October)

OCTOBER 1988

24 MONDAY

The inventor of the ballpoint pen for handwriting died three years ago today. Señor Ladislao Biro ensured that his name would always be remembered when he decided to find an alternative to the leaky, unreliable fountain pen. When the first Biros arrived in Britain they sold for £2 15s each.

And did you know that . . .
No one knows the secret recipe of the varnish used by Anton Stradivario on his violins?
*   An American has patented special boots with pockets to make life easier for nudists?*

25 TUESDAY

Today in France in 1984 the fifth 'Marianne' was selected. The Marianne is a bust of a young French woman, the symbol of the French Republic, and it's displayed in town halls in France. The latest woman to be chosen for the honour is Catherine Deneuve; her officially-approved bust joins that of Brigitte Bardot, the fourth Marianne.

And did you know that . . .
According to mathematicians, whenever twenty-three people gather together there is a more than 50 per cent chance that two of them will share the same birthday?

26 WEDNESDAY

Jackie Coogan, the first child-star to earn a million dollars, was born today in 1914. Introduced to movies by Charlie Chaplin, he went on to found his own production company and had earned $2 million by the time he was 10. When he came of age at 21 he found his mother and stepfather had taken the lot and left him in debt. The outrage led to a bill to protect the rights of child performers.

And did you know that . . .
Horror writer Edgar Allan Poe used to write with a black cat sitting on his shoulder?

27 THURSDAY

John Cleese is 49 today. He's probably most famous for his TV portrayal of Basil Fawlty, proprietor of the worst-run guest-house in the country. When 'Fawlty Towers' was sold to Spain there were worries about what the audience would make of Manuel, the put-upon Spanish waiter. The problem was solved by making Manuel Italian.

OCTOBER 1988

28 FRIDAY

74 years ago today Jonas Salk was born. He went on to produce a vaccine against one of the world's most debilitating diseases, polio. Within ten years of his discovery the number of polio victims had been reduced by 95 per cent.

And did you know that . . .

The Statue of Liberty's nose is 4ft 6in long?

James Garfield was the only ambidextrous US President?

The avocado tree is so prolific that some trees have been known to collapse under the sheer weight of the fruit they bear?

29 SATURDAY

Champion jockey Lester Piggott retired from racing three years ago today. He went out on a high note with his 4,349th winner and told everyone that after 30 years of living on the verge of starvation he was looking forward to being able to eat again.

And did you know that . . .

The cost of building the Eiffel Tower was completely recouped in visitors' entrance fees a year after it had been finished?

The turkey got its name after British settlers in North America decided that its profile looked like a map of Turkey?

30 SUNDAY

Julia McArdle made an appearance in court four years ago today and had her father to thank for the £100 fine she received for failing a breath test. Her father, Geoffrey McArdle, was the inventor of the machine that registered she was over the limit.

And did you know that . . .

President Abraham Lincoln's body has been moved 17 times to prevent its theft?

There is a fish which is known by the scientific classification Boops Boops?

NOTES

On Humour...

When it comes to British humour I was a great fan of 'The Goon Show'. I had a facility for doing all the voices that Peter Sellers did on the show and if he was down I'd start doing them. He'd say, 'No, that's not right,' and correct me and that would get him going. If anyone invited him to dinner they used to invite me along too!

(27 October)

OCTOBER 1988

31
MONDAY

Today is Hallowe'en, which is derived from the ancient Celtic festival of Samain. During this time ghosts and witches were said to roam the earth. On the same day the Romans worshipped the goddess of orchards, Pomona, which may explain the origin of apple-bobbing. The Christian church couldn't ignore these traditions and so in AD835 they rededicated them to the saints in heaven and called the next day All Saints' Day.

And did you know that . . .
During the average lifetime the heart pumps enough blood to fill the fuel tanks of more than 2,000 Boeing 747 airliners?

NOTES

_____

_____

_____

_____

_____

_____

THINGS TO DO IN NOVEMBER:

_____

_____

_____

_____

_____

_____

_____

_____

NOVEMBER 1988

1 TUESDAY

ERNIE is 32 today! The Electronic Random Number Indicator Equipment was introduced in 1956 by the Post Office to assist in the task of selecting winning premium bond numbers.

And did you know that . . .

A Russian woman has developed X-ray vision after receiving a massive electric shock?

The Icelandic language has remained almost entirely unchanged since the twelfth century?

2 WEDNESDAY

Burt Lancaster, star of *Elmer Gantry, Airport* and *Local Hero* is 75 today. Before he came to be a Hollywood actor he was a circus acrobat.

And did you know that . . .

At least one third of Moroccan carpet factory workers are under the age of 12?

In May 1919 only five rainy days were recorded?

In Spain some cows were given false stainless steel teeth?

It's been calculated that two octopuses can kiss in more than a million different ways?

3 THURSDAY

31 years ago a Samoyed dog called Laika was launched in Sputnik II and became the first living creature in space. Sadly, she wasn't the first living creature to return from space: she died when her oxygen supply ran out after 10 days.

And did you know that . . .

Prince Dolgoroucki of Russia was killed while participating in a strange duel? He and his opponent agreed to stand in the front line of their army until one of them was shot down by a cannonball.

If all the tubes in the liver were laid end to end they would stretch a distance of 95 kilometres?

NOVEMBER 1988

4 FRIDAY

66 years ago today Howard Carter and Lord Carnarvon discovered the tomb of Egyptian boy-king Tutankhamen. It had taken 16 years and cost more than £200,000 by the time they uncovered the tomb door with its inscription, 'Lo. I am here.'

More recently, in 1984 to be precise, four American male tourists were charged with indecency after removing their clothing and posing naked for photos outside the Parthenon, Athens.

And did you know that . . .
Before Charles Bronson became a star he was a coalminer?

5 SATURDAY

According to a national survey carried out two years ago, the ideal restaurant meal consists of prawn cocktail, steak and chips and chocolate gateau.

Six years ago the stuffed body of Guy the Gorilla, one of London Zoo's favourites, was put on display in the Museum of Natural History.

And did you know that . . .
Al Capone's visiting card gave his profession as 'secondhand furniture dealer'?

6 SUNDAY

Four years ago today reports came in from Belgrade that 30 people from a remote Yugoslavian village were in hospital after eating badger meat, which superstition said would cure asthma and other breathing problems.

And did you know that . . .
The song 'White Christmas' does not come from the film White Christmas *but from* Holiday Inn?
When 100 schoolchildren were asked to name the world's most beautiful woman – 61 chose Joan Collins and 4 their mothers?

NOTES

On the Big Break...

My big break was *Alfie*. It was *Alfie* that got me noticed in the USA. That was 20 years ago and lots of people still think of me as Alfie. Cab drivers still yell it at me! Because of the role I played in the film people *still* have this image of me as a male chauvinist. I'm not, but no one will believe it!　　(2 November)

NOVEMBER 1988

7
MONDAY

14 years ago today Lord Lucan disappeared after, it is presumed, he had battered his children's nanny to death. Most of his friends believe that he committed suicide but the police are keeping the files open. Each year brings new sightings; in 1978 he was spotted in Melbourne, Holland, Dublin and Johannesburg – simultaneously!

And did you know that . . .
The last sea battle in which all the ships had sails occurred in the Bay of Navarino off Greece in 1826?

8
TUESDAY

Four years ago news came from Montreal that a cinema usher was claiming the world record for boredom after sitting through 57 consecutive showings of *Bedtime For Bonzo*, starring Ronald Reagan and a chimpanzee. His reward for this amazing feat? A copy of the film.

88 years ago Margaret Mitchell, author of *Gone with The Wind*, was born. Not many people know that in her original book the glamorous Scarlett O'Hara was called Pansy.

And did you know that . . .
The Roman Emperor Claudius choked to death on a feather that his doctor had stuck down his throat in an attempt to make him vomit up some poisoned food he'd just swallowed?

9
WEDNESDAY

Wonderful, witty, tough-talking Katharine Hepburn is 79 today! While she was making *The Lion in Winter*, for which she won a Best Actress Oscar, a journalist noticed that she was wearing training shoes under her twelfth-century robes and asked her why. Miss Hepburn told him, 'I play Queen Eleanor of Aquitaine, Queen of England – and also a practical woman who believed in comfort.'

And did you know that . . .
A young Harpy eagle ready to leave its nest is bigger than its parents, who have exhausted themselves feeding it?

10
THURSDAY

Today in 1925 Richard Burton was born. When Burton first went to Hollywood he was ignored by almost everyone; in fact if he hadn't married Elizabeth Taylor he might never have become internationally famous. At Miss Taylor's sixth wedding she was asked by the official conducting the ceremony to name her previous husbands. 'What's this,' she asked, ' a memory test?'

NOVEMBER 1988

11
FRIDAY

Today in 1981 an armistice was signed between the inhabitants of a Spanish village and Denmark. In 1809 the leaders of the village, called Huescar, were appalled to learn that Denmark had sided with France against Britain in the Napoleonic Wars. They declared war on Denmark, although the Danish never knew about it, and it took 172 years for peace to be officially restored.

And did you know that . . .
Redheads have fewer hairs on their heads than blondes or brunettes?

12
SATURDAY

55 years ago today the first photo of the Loch Ness monster was snapped, by Mr Hugh Gray. He managed to take five pictures before Nessie slipped away, but after processing, four of them were blank. The fifth showed an object that might or might not have been a monster, though some suspected that it was only a tree trunk.

And did you know that . . .
Doc Holliday died with his boots on? His final words were to a nurse who'd just taken them off: 'Damn it, put 'em back on!'

13
SUNDAY

Four years ago it was reported in Washington that a robber had held up a Chinese laundry and fired a shot from his gun to frighten the workers there. Unfortunately it didn't work; he blasted himself through the foot.

70 years ago today the bra was patented by Mary Phelps Jacob and not by the legendary Otto Titzling, as widely believed.

And did you know that . . .
Oscar Wilde wrote 'The Ballad of Reading Gaol' under the name C.3.3., meaning the prisoner in Cell 3, on the prison's third landing?

NOTES

On Favourite Film Stars...

My favourite actor is Humphrey Bogart, without a doubt. Katharine Hepburn is an actress I much admire, but my favourite of all was Bette Davis. There were others I fancied, like Ruth Roman, but Bogart and Davis are magic.   (9 November)

NOVEMBER 1988

14
MONDAY

Six years ago elections were held in Albania. There was a 100 per cent turnout of the 1,627,968 people eligible to take part and only one person cast their vote against the ruling Communist Party.

And did you know that . . .
Penguins have about seventy feathers per square inch?
Around one in ten autistic children, who cannot communicate normally, possesses extraordinary talent for music, memorization or mathematics?
The Statue of Liberty's torch was originally lit with a bonfire?

15
TUESDAY

53 years ago today that great Marx Brothers comedy *A Night at the Opera* received its première in New York. Another of their movies, *A Night in Casablanca*, got them into trouble with Warner Brothers who thought the title was too close to their own *Casablanca* and threatened to sue. Groucho responded by threatening, 'I'll sue you for using the word *Brothers*.'

And did you know that . . .
Louis Blériot was the first man to enter Britain without arriving by sea?

16
WEDNESDAY

10 years ago today the most northerly island in the world was discovered. Measuring only two hundred yards square and consisting of frozen rock, it lies north of Greenland.

And did you know that . . .
Some parts of Eire are north of Northern Ireland?
Most centipedes do not have a hundred legs?
In 1974 the firefly was declared the official insect of Pennsylvania?
St Francis of Rome is the patron saint of bachelors?

17
THURSDAY

The late Rock Hudson was born today in 1925. Not many people know that he was born Roy Scherer and his agent invented his new name, basing it on the River Hudson and the Rock of Gibraltar.

And did you know that . . .
There are more chickens than people in England?
The waiting rooms at one of Peking's railway stations can hold around 14,000 people?

NOVEMBER 1988

18
FRIDAY

Mickey Mouse is 60 today! The greatest cartoon character ever created, he's received more fan mail than any human movie star, appeared in more than a hundred films, won an Oscar and travelled the world. Not bad for a character who was originally dreamed up after Walt Disney found mice nesting in his waste paper basket!

And did you know that . . .
The earliest shorthand system on record was devised by a Roman in 63BC for recording speeches in the Senate?

19
SATURDAY

10 years ago today in Guyana the 900 members of the People's Temple religious sect, lead by Jim Jones, committed suicide by swallowing soft drinks mixed with cyanide. Jones died of gunshot wounds, leaving $7 million to aid 'the oppressed people of the world'.

And did you know that . . .
Shirley Temple was originally intended to play the part that eventually went to Judy Garland in The Wizard of Oz?
The Dobermann dog is named after Louis Dobermann, who created the breed?

20
SUNDAY

Four years ago a report from Moscow revealed that men were scouring the city looking for western-style trousers with zips. All the trouser-making factories were turning out trousers with button flies.
82 years ago today Mr Rolls got together with Mr Royce and formed the company that still makes the most prestigious and luxurious cars in the world.

And did you know that . . .
If Father Christmas visits each house on earth on Christmas Eve he must travel faster than 50,000 miles per second?

NOTES

On Groucho Marx...

I knew Groucho Marx very well. He was madly in love with Shakira, my wife – he was around 85 years old at the time. Every time I met him at a party I'd walk in and say, 'Hallo Groucho' and he'd say, 'Hallo Michael, hallo, Shakira. Would you get me a drink, Michael?' I'd go off to get him whatever he wanted and the minute I left the room he'd get out of his wheelchair, grab Shakira, kiss her and sit down in the wheelchair very quickly!

(15 November)

NOVEMBER 1988

21
MONDAY

14 years ago today that real-life Reginald Perrin, John Stonehouse, went for a dip in the sea off Miami and disappeared, believed drowned. A year later he was spotted in Australia with his secretary Sheila Buckley on his arm. Fraud trials and a divorce from Mrs Stonehouse followed shortly.

And did you know that . . .
The windows of the NASA space probe to Venus were made of diamond?

22
TUESDAY

25 years ago today John F. Kennedy was shot as he travelled in his Lincoln car through the streets of Dallas, Texas. During the autopsy that followed his brain was removed and lost, and he had to be buried without it.

And did you know that . . .
Elephant polo is a real sport?
More Americans can trace their ancestors back to Germany than to any other country?

23
WEDNESDAY

'Dr Who', the world's longest-running TV science fiction serial, was first broadcast 25 years ago today. Among Doctor Who's most fearsome enemies are the Daleks, whose ambition is to rule the world. This seems unlikely – the Daleks can't even climb stairs!

And did you know that . . .
Nigeria is one of the few countries that still, like the UK, has a hard-cover passport?
The Great Wall of China stretches for approximately one-twentieth of the world's circumference?

24
THURSDAY

The ill-fated saga of John De Lorean and his shiny aluminium gull-wing cars came to an end six years ago today at an auction where dealers paid as much as £15,000 to buy themselves a piece of motoring history. And they weren't able to drive themselves home in their De Loreans afterwards – the cars didn't meet British safety standards.

And did you know that . . .
The American postal system is the busiest in the world?
The Tinguian tribe of the Philippines have developed flutes which they play with their noses?

NOVEMBER 1988

25 FRIDAY

26 years ago today *The Mousetrap*, the longest-running play in the world, opened in London. Agatha Christie was quite pleased with the production and predicted that it might run for eighteen months.

And did you know that . . .

The British navy lost its rum ration in 1973?

 After 1503 Popes were not allowed to have children? Before then, many had been married and acknowledged their children.

 According to scientists, the Earth is shrinking by about 0·1 of a millimetre each year?

26 SATURDAY

Today is the fortieth birthday of Charles M. Schulz, creator of Snoopy. His *Peanuts* cartoon strip is the most widely read in the world.

And did you know that . . .

A 1981 survey of the contents of a hundred executives' briefcases revealed that most of them carried nothing more than a newspaper or magazine, their lunch and a bottle of aftershave?

 Aspirin is not addictive?

 The Statue of Liberty's index finger is eight feet long?

27 SUNDAY

There was bad news in Communist China four years ago today. The two-hour lunch break was officially abolished.

And did you know that . . .

'Angels on horseback' is a savoury of bacon-wrapped prunes.

 The common teazle is still used in industry to brush knitted fabric and raise the pile of woven cloth?

 A hump-backed whale can travel more than 6,400 miles in its annual migrations?

NOTES

On Communism and Russian Spies...

I'm fascinated by the world of spies and espionage, and not just because I played Harry Palmer. I once met a Russian diplomat and we went out drinking and got talking. When I started to say something about England he said, 'You have nothing to say about Britain, we destroyed you 20 years ago.' And as we found out with Burgess, Philby, Maclean and Blunt, he was right.

(27 November)

NOVEMBER 1988

28 MONDAY

11 years ago today John Winslow yo-yoed for 120 hours and earned a place in the record books. In 1933, when the first yo-yo craze was at its height, Damascus was hit by a terrible drought. Muslim leaders met to discuss the crisis and came to the conclusion that the lack of water was caused by the constant movement of thousands of yo-yos. Immediately an order went out banning them. The next day it rained.

And did you know that . . .
Haydn's 'Miracle' symphony is so called because during one performance a chandelier crashed to the floor, injuring no one?

29 TUESDAY

Composer Gaetano Donizetti was born today in 1797 and in his 50-year life composed an amazing 60 operas. In his haste he sometimes failed to research his subjects properly and as a result one of his works is set in the romantic-sounding 'mountains near Liverpool'.

And did you know that . . .
The movie Thirteen Women *has only ten female stars?*
A fifteenth-century law banning all Jews from Spain was only repealed in 1968?

30 WEDNESDAY

52 years ago today the Crystal Palace was destroyed by a blaze so hot that its acres of glass melted and fell in drops. An estimated four million people turned out to see the spectacle but amazingly no one was killed.

And did you know that . . .
Romeo and Juliet *was performed in Tibetan for the first time in 1981?*
Santiago in Chile was the last major city with a population of more than four million to rely on a volunteer fire service?

NOTES

_____

_____

THINGS TO DO IN DECEMBER:

_____

_____

THE STRESS-FREE CALENDAR

Trying to pack too many jobs and engagements into a single month can lead to stress — and when you're stressed you're not at your best. Fortunately there's a solution; the Stress-Free Calendar. It's a special alternative calendar for handling those difficult months, like December, when there are a million things to do and not enough time for half of them.

★ In business everyone want things done yesterday. The Stress-Free Calendar allows you to discuss a deal on the 22nd and reach a decision on the 21st.

★ Because everyone wants things wrapped up by Friday there are two Fridays each week.

★ There's an extra week added to each month to allow you to fit a few more things in.

★ As a general rule Mondays aren't very productive, so they are abolished and replaced by Negotiationday, thus allowing the rest of the week to be kept free for work.

★ Saturdays have been scrapped because they're usually a waste of time and leave you with a hangover on Sunday. Sundays have been retained on the grounds that everyone needs one day off each week.

★ To relieve any stress on the superstitions, Friday the 13th has been removed from the calendar.

SUN	FRI	FRI	THUR	WED	TUE	NEG
7	6	5	4	3	2	1
15	14	12	11	10	9	8
22	21	20	19	18	17	16
29	28	27	26	25	24	23
36	35	34	33	32	31	30
					38	37

DECEMBER 1988

1
THURSDAY

Happy birthday to Woody Allen, 53 today! Woody's hallmark is his personal brand of paranoia. He worries about everything, including death. 'It's not that I'm afraid to die. I just don't want to be there when it happens,' he once told a journalist.

And did you know that . . .

The last eye-witness to see the assassination of President Lincoln died in 1956?

After it had been struck off with five blows of the axe, the head of James Duke of Monmouth was sewn back on so that his portrait could be painted?

DECEMBER 1988

2
FRIDAY

Eight years ago today a Danish shipping clerk and his cat won £68,000 on the Danish football pools. The cat had assisted by batting a dice with its paws while its owner recorded the results on his pools form.

And did you know that . . .

The CIA once employed a magician to write a book teaching agents how to use sleight of hand in their work?
Llamas can wiggle each ear independently?
The magnolia tree is named after botanist Pierre Magnol?

3
SATURDAY

21 years ago today Louis Washkansky made history by becoming the first transplant patient to receive a human heart successfully. The operation was performed by Dr Christiaan Barnard, took just over three hours and had almost immediate results. Sadly Mr Washkansky died from a lung infection after 18 days, but his new heart kept beating to the end.

And did you know that . . .

In a 1986 survey of favourite foods, vegetable soup was declared to be the most popular flavour?

4
SUNDAY

11 years ago today Jean-Bedel Bokassa crowned himself Emperor of the Central African Republic. Despite the fact that his country was one of the poorest in the world he spent £16,000,000 on the ceremony and celebrations, £3 million of it on his imperial crown.

And did you know that . . .

Leonardo da Vinci is believed to have had a condition called 'double hemisphere action'? People with this condition can write different sentences with both right and left hands while at the same time carrying on a conversation with someone else.

NOTES

On Woody Allen...

I enjoyed working with Woody Allen. He's very professional and when you work with him you don't go into the studio and have a laugh. It's a very serious, quiet set when you work with Woody, a bit like acting in church. Comedy is a serious business. A *very* serious business.

(1 December)

DECEMBER 1988

5
MONDAY

197 years ago today Mozart died aged only 35. During his short life he wrote an amazing 600 pieces – but then he had started young. At the age of seven he wrote his first sonata and a year later he'd completed his first symphony.

And did you know that . . .
The Yucatan peninsula is so called because when explorers first reached the area they asked the Indians what it was called. 'Yucatan,' said the Indians, and the explorers adopted the name. How were they to know 'yucatan' means, 'What do you mean?'

6
TUESDAY

Today in 1926 mysterious black snow fell in France. No one was able to offer an explanation for it.

Today is also St Nicholas's Day. He's the patron saint of schoolboys, virgins, Turkey, Greece, sailors and thieves.

And did you know that . . .
A British medical journal reported the case of a woman who had been regularly drinking Dettol over a period of years in an attempt to 'purify' herself?

7
WEDNESDAY

17 years ago today the publishing company McGraw-Hill announced a major coup; they had bought the rights to the autobiography of Howard Hughes, who had for many years been a recluse. 'We are absolutely certain of the authenticity of this autobiography,' declared a company executive. Just four months later it was revealed that the whole thing was a hoax dreamed up by Clifford Irving.

And did you know that . . .
The only animal whose evidence is admissible in a court of law is a bloodhound?

8
THURSDAY

Eight years ago today John Lennon was shot by Mark Chapman, a 25-year-old who had earlier asked for his autograph. Radio stations throughout the USA started playing non-stop Beatles records, and thousands gathered outside the Dakota apartment building where Lennon and Yoko Ono had been buying up flats; they owned at least five.

DECEMBER 1988

9 FRIDAY

Forget 'Dallas' and 'East Enders'; *'Coronation Street'*, the greatest soap opera of them all, was first broadcast 28 years ago today. On the subject of soap operas, Rudolph Hess is reported to be a keen fan of 'Dynasty'.

And did you know that . . .

Alan Pinkerton, founder of the famous US detective agency, died of gangrene of the tongue after tripping and biting it while out on a morning stroll?

Benjamin Disraeli's false teeth once fell out while he was talking in Parliament?

10 SATURDAY

According to H.L. Mencken the first bathtub to arrive in America was unveiled today at a special party. It wasn't. The whole story was made up.

And did you know that . . .

In 1984 a team of 12-year-olds beat a team of Westminster MPs in a chess tournament?

Che Guevara suffered from asthma?

The Old Testament contains 592,439 words.

11 SUNDAY

At 10 p.m. 52 years ago today Edward VIII announced his abdication to the nation. All normal activities came to a halt as listeners tuned in on their radios to hear him explain that he 'found it impossible to carry the heavy burden of responsibility... without the help of the woman I love.' He had reigned for 325 days.

And did you know that . . .

In the days before British Rail the Midland and Great Northern line became known as 'The Muddle and Get Nowhere Line'?

NOTES

On John Lennon...

I knew John Lennon. During the Sixties we were all around in London – the Beatles, the Rolling Stones. There was none of this reclusiveness like you get now. John was very, very clever with a cutting kind of wit. If you got on the wrong side of him he could be very sharp. Fortunately I was never on the receiving end of it!

(8 December)

DECEMBER 1988

12 MONDAY

Three years ago the extraordinary case of the Russian sleeper was in the headlines. Mr Vladimir Leontov, a Russian who was living in France, was taken to hospital after an accident on a British road. After being refused a single room, a cooker and a nurse to read Byron to him he dropped off – and refused to wake up again. Eventually he was shipped back to France, still snoozing.

And did you know that . . .
When he became the first man to step on the Moon, Neil Armstrong was wearing size 9½ space boots?

13 TUESDAY

411 years ago today Sir Francis Drake set off on his round-the-world voyage. More than 400 years later a modern yachtsman decided to follow his example and asked experts to recommend the lightest and most nutritious food he could carry with him. They told him to take moist, pre-packed dog food.

And did you know that . . .
After spending £1 million in 1982 to launch their new Lymeswold cheese, the Milk Marketing Board had to spend thousands more explaining why it couldn't supply the demand?
Hamburgers were once prescribed as a cure for people suffering from anaemia and asthma?

14 WEDNESDAY

59 years ago today the world's first miniature golf course was opened in Tennessee.
70 years ago British women voted in a General Election for the first time.

And did you know that . . .
Hundreds of thousands of banknotes were issued in Yugoslavia in December 1985, each carrying a picture of President Tito and the wrong date of his death?

15 THURSDAY

44 years ago today band leader Glenn Miller, who had been in England entertaining the troops, climbed into a light plane for the trip across the Channel to Paris. He questioned the fact that there were no parachutes on board. 'What's the matter, Miller?' asked the pilot. 'You want to live for ever?' The plane took off but never arrived in Paris, nor was any wreckage ever found.

DECEMBER 1988

16
FRIDAY

Noël Coward, playwright and actor, was born today in 1899. Famed in later life for his wit and manners, he was an appallingly behaved child. Once he stole books from the Army and Navy stores, and another time he poured a kettle of boiling water down the ear-trumpet of a deaf hall porter.

And did you know that . . .

In 1147 Pope Eugene III was to arrive in Paris on a Friday, a fast-day; to allow people to feast instead, he decreed that that Friday would be a Thursday, giving two in one week.

17
SATURDAY

88 years ago today a reward was announced for the first person to communicate with extra-terrestrial beings. However, communication with Martians didn't count because they were believed to be too easy to contact.

And did you know that . . .

There have only been two bald presidents of the USA?
Llamas have bad breath?
A camel's feet are soft and silky?

18
SUNDAY

66 years ago today a Sussex solicitor discovered an ancient skull at Piltdown. The archeological world said it was certainly the 'missing link', and it became internationally famous as Piltdown Man. Then in 1953 scientists discovered that it was a fake, created from a human cranium and an orang-utan's jaw.

And did you know that . . .

Dr Kellogg, who invented cornflakes, also invented peanut butter?
Vampire bats most often bite the ears, nose or toes of human victims?
George VI, Mozart and Casanova were all Freemasons?

NOTES

On Noël Coward...

I made a picture with Noël Coward, *The Italian Job*. We were very good friends and I think the most English thing I ever used to do in my life was have dinner with him every Wednesday at the Savoy for the 12 or 14 weeks we were making the film. He actually mentions me in his diaries, very nicely, I'm proud of that.   (16 December)

DECEMBER 1988

19 MONDAY

French chanteuse Edith Piaf was born today in 1915 and spent most of her early life living in a brothel.

And today in 1958 President Eisenhower wished the world a special merry Christmas. His message was relayed around the world via a satellite for the first time.

And did you know that . . .
Cocoa beans were once used as currency by the Mayans?
Oslo used to be known as Christiana?
Field Marshal Viscount Montgomery was a vegetarian?

20 TUESDAY

Uri Geller, spoon-bender and mind reader, is 42 today. He discovered his incredible powers at the age of sixteen when he began to read his mother's mind and for his first day at school he was given a watch which never worked properly because every time he looked at it the hands started spinning wildly.

And did you know that . . .
The average lead pencil will write 50,000 words before running out?
The youngest golfer to have scored a hole in one is Corby Orr who achieved the feat at the age of five?

21 WEDNESDAY

75 years ago today the world's first crossword puzzle appeared in the New York *World*. There were no black squares and the grid was arranged in a diamond shape.

And did you know that . . .
Harpo Marx liked to greet visitors to his house in the nude?
People who have seen Abominable Snow-women say that their breasts are so large they can fling them over their shoulders?
After Blackbeard the pirate had been killed, his murderers cut off his beard and flew it from their mast?

22 THURSDAY

The coelacanth made a surprise return today in 1938 – surprising because it was believed to have been extinct for 70 million years. The Anjouan islanders where the second specimen was found weren't surprised at all. They'd been using the coelacanth's rough scales for years – to repair punctures in their bicycle tyres..

DECEMBER 1988

23 FRIDAY

A survey published three years ago today revealed that the average family with children spent £265 on presents for Christmas 1984.

Today in Oaxaca, Mexico, they're holding the annual radish fiesta. For 200 years gigantic radishes have been bought, sold, and carved into amazing shapes. Prizes are awarded for the most imaginative carvings.

And did you know that . . .
In the fifteenth century Chinese scholars produced an encyclopaedia with 11,000 volumes?

24 SATURDAY

Howard Hughes was born today in 1905. Having inherited oil money from his father he went on to blow millions of it on making second-rate movies. Chauffeurs who drove his female starlets around were instructed not to go faster than 2 mph in case a bumpy ride ruined the firmness of their breasts.

And did you know that . . .
The composer Tchaikovsky tried to commit suicide by standing all night in a freezing river?

25 SUNDAY

What do Princess Alexandra, Sir Isaac Newton, Kenny Everett, Little Richard and Humphrey Bogart have in common? All of them were born on Christmas Day!

And did you know that . . .
There's a town called Santa Claus in Indiana, USA?
*   Oliver Cromwell passed a law decreeing that anyone found making or eating mince pies and Christmas pudding was liable to a fine or spell in prison?*

NOTES

25 December: *Christmas Day — Public holiday in Great Britain and Northern Ireland.*

On Christmas Presents . . .

The best Christmas present I ever had was a banana, because during the war (I was six when it started) you couldn't get bananas or oranges. At Christmas they used to ferry these boats across the sea, past all the U-boats and German destroyers, with fruit for the kids. One Christmas every child got an orange and a banana. It was the first banana I'd ever tasted.

DECEMBER 1988

26
MONDAY

Boxing Day is named after an old custom in which apprentices would visit their masters' customers, clutching a box marked TIP – To Insure Punctuality. Hence the word 'tip'.

A hundred years ago today the West End saw the shortest-ever run of a play. It was called *The Lady of Lyons* and the audience flocked to the Shaftesbury Theatre to see it. After waiting for an hour they were told to go away because the safety curtain wouldn't open. The following day the play was cancelled.

27
TUESDAY

Three years ago today the Chinese News Agency revealed that the best-selling book of the year in China was a sex manual.

The world's most glamorous grandmother, Marlene Dietrich, is 87 today. Courted by the rich and famous, she turned down the chance to be Hitler's mistress and at the age of eighty still retained her hourglass figure.

And did you know that . . .
Tenoroons, hecklephones and bombarons are all types of woodwind instrument?

28
WEDNESDAY

Today in 1869 chewing gum was patented by William Finley Semple. Before long it was being used for purposes even he couldn't have predicted. The airship R-34 sprang a leak in one of its engines during the journey across the Atlantic. Some quick thinking – and chewing – saved the day and the hole was plugged with gum.

And did you know that . . .
Lettuce is the only common vegetable that is not sold frozen, tinned, bottled, processed or pre-cooked?

29
THURSDAY

Today in 1170 St Thomas à Becket was murdered in Canterbury Cathedral. Underneath his archbishop's regalia he was found to be wearing an itchy hair shirt, crawling with lice, as a penance.

And did you know that . . .
The so-called black panther is actually a leopard?
India ink isn't made in India? It comes from China.
The comma was introduced to the English language in about 1520?
Elizabeth Taylor never throws any of her clothes away?

DECEMBER 1988

FRIDAY

The indestructible mad monk Rasputin finally died 72 years ago today – though it took a lot to kill him. When cakes spiced with cyanide had no effect on him his would-be murderers shot him several times and battered him with a truncheon. Then they tied him up tightly and flung him in the ice-covered river. When the body was recovered several days later he had pulled one arm free of the ropes, proving that it had been the water and not the assassins that had finished him off.

And did you know that . . .
Pigs are very poor swimmers?

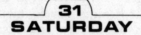
SATURDAY

135 years ago today in London 21 scientists were guests at a select dinner party held inside a lifesize model of an iguanadon. Today is also Hogmanay, which is celebrated north of the border despite the fact that no one is certain what the word actually means. One suggestion is that it's taken from the ancient Greek phrase *Hagia-mana*, meaning 'Holy Month'.

And did you know that . . .
Women have a better sense of taste than men?

NOTES

26 December: *Boxing Day — Public holiday in Great Britain and Northern Ireland.*

On Marlene Dietrich...

I sat next to Marlene Dietrich at dinner once and she told me I should dress better. She did nothing but lecture me all through dinner. She said I should have worn a tie! Peter Sellers came up and when he went away she said, 'Do you know that dreadful man?' She hated Peter Sellers. I don't know why... (27 December)

_____

_____

THINGS TO DO IN 1988:

_____

_____

_____

The National Playing Fields Association

Sixty years ago the National Playing Fields Association was established with a simple mandate: every child has a right to play. Nothing could be simpler. Yet our society is losing sight of this simple idea.

The NPFA has not, and is now one of the most effective voices for better play provision. It is not a fashionable cause. Nor is it an emotional cause. It is a cause concerned with the bed-rock on which our society is founded.

We live in a world designed and built for adults by adults. Children must live in this world too. It is the world in which they have to grow. A vital part of that growing-up process is play. For children, play is not trivial or unimportant. It is an integral part of their healthy development. It is in their play that children learn about life and about living — their preparation for their future. Without it, the deprived child develops into the deprived adult. Children need to play and have the right to grow and develop in freedom and in safety.

A concern for how children grow and develop is a concern for the future and the shape our society will take. The NPFA believes that we are failing our children, ourselves and our future in this key area. But it is still not too late, though the call for action grows more urgent.

We call our world 'the developed world'. How do children see it? They see: high rise flats; estates with postage-stamp gardens; signs which say 'Keep off the Grass' and 'No Ball Games Here'; more space for cars than for children. It is not just the environment which has become alien, almost hostile, to children, but people as well. We have separated children from adults in their work, their education and their leisure.

We are destroying their play world. We are placing our children at risk and in doing so we place our future at risk. The simple needs are often forgotten.

The Real Needs

In providing real play opportunities we can no longer salve our consciences by giving expensive toys and play equipment. Just to provide swings and roundabouts is only scratching at the surface of children's real needs. It is not just a question of space and equipment. Children also need:

　　to be creative
　　to be stimulated and challenged
　　to be involved in all aspects of life.

Otherwise they will seek their excitement in other ways.

Most of all the NPFA believes children need people. Children need the care and involvement of adults in their play. This means nothing less than a total change of attitudes. Bringing children — and their play — into the centre of our lives and thinking.

When we plan for children we plan for our future. The NPFA believes this means fighting for children:

> fighting to give them space
> fighting to give them time to play
> fighting to give them opportunities for play
> fighting to involve people in their play.

Above all else, the NPFA is fighting for the child's right to play. It means making the right choices in allocating our national resources. Play is cost effective:

> it saves — repairing children's bodies and minds
> it saves — by lessening delinquency, violence and vandalism
> it saves — by preventing stress in families.

That is what the NPFA's appeal for children's play is about. It is the only organization with the potential to fight effectively for children's play. We urgently need your help and support:

> to create a greater understanding of the value of play to children
> to persuade both public and private sectors of their responsibilities to children
> to improve the quantity and quality of play opportunities for children
> to support means of involving adults in the play — and therefore the lives of children
> to search for new initiatives for children's play provision.

In fact:
TO FIGHT FOR THE CHILD'S RIGHT TO PLAY.

If you would like to help, this is the address to write to:

The National Playing Fields Association,
25 Ovington Square,
London SW3 1LQ.
Telephone: 01-584 6445.